✳

# THE SKY IS NOT
# THE
# LIMIT

## ALSO BY NEIL DE GRASSE TYSON

MERLIN'S TOUR OF THE UNIVERSE

UNIVERSE DOWN TO EARTH

JUST VISITING THIS PLANET

ONE UNIVERSE: AT HOME IN THE COSMOS
*(with Charles Liu and Robert Irion)*

# THE SKY IS NOT
# THE
# LIMIT

## ADVENTURES OF AN URBAN
## ASTROPHYSICIST

## Neil de Grasse Tyson

**DOUBLEDAY**
New York London Toronto Sydney Auckland

PUBLISHED BY DOUBLEDAY
A division of Random House, Inc.
1540 Broadway, New York, New York 10036

DOUBLEDAY and the portrayal of an anchor with a dolphin are
trademarks of Doubleday, a division of Random House, Inc.

DESIGNED BY LISA SLOANE

Excerpt from "Hold Fast to Dreams" from *Collected Poems* by
Langston Hughes, © 1994 by the Estate of Langston Hughes.
Reprinted by permission of Alfred A. Knopf,
a division of Random House, Inc.

Library of Congress Cataloging-in-Publication Data
Tyson, Neil de Grasse.
The sky is not the limit: adventures of an urban
astrophysicist/Neil de Grasse Tyson.—1st ed.
p.      cm.
1. Tyson, Neil de Grasse.   2. Astrophysicists—United States—
Biography. I. Title.
QB460.T97 2000
523.01´092—dc21
[B]
99-049904
CIP

ISBN 0-385-48838-6

1 3 5 7 9 10 8 6 4 2

FOR MIRANDA

*In the hope that the star for which she reaches*
*Sits higher and brighter than any I have known.*

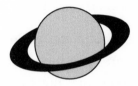

# PREFACE

MEMOIRS ARE SIMULTANEOUSLY EASY AND HARD TO WRITE. For me, the material was all there—the details of my scientific journeys were either recovered from my memory or retrieved from rather extensive records I have kept throughout my life. Surely it would be easy to assemble the interesting parts and write about them.

But I am neither a movie star, a sports celebrity, nor an important political figure. These professions make fertile lifestyles for the memoir format and typically attract wide readership. In my case, I am just a scientist—an astrophysicist—who has tried to bring the universe down to Earth for everybody who wanted to see it. Along the way, I have also tried to raise public literacy in science a notch or two. I consider it a privilege to do so.

Why then might you be interested in my story?

In these pages, I share with the reader many amusing (and playful) pedagogical moments. But I especially share the segments of my life's paths that got me here, which, for the most part, were upstream and against the winds of society. The paths include fond memories of mentors (the only people whose names I mention), some of whom were ordinary people doing extraordinary things while others were extraordinary people doing ordinary things. The paths further include the retelling of some traumatic moments where my will, my life's goals, and my sense of identity were tested to their limits.

Regardless of what you may seek in my or anyone else's memoir, I can promise you that *The Sky Is Not the Limit* will bring you closer to the universe of ambition; and, as is my duty, bring you closer to the universe itself.

NEIL DE GRASSE TYSON
New York City
January 2000

# Contents

*Beyond the judgments of others*
*Rising high above the sky*
*Lies the power of ambition*

*—NDT*

# THE SKY IS NOT THE
# THE
# LIMIT

# INTRODUCTION

At my high school's twentieth-year reunion, during the obliga-
tory assessments of how well time had treated us all, I won the
"the coolest job" contest in a straw poll of all those attending.
That particular graduating class from New York City's Bronx
High School of Science was not unusual. It had produced the
typical ensemble of scientists, medical doctors, lawyers, and
the like. But I was the only one who had keys to the candy
store, so who was I to argue the honor? As an astrophysicist
and as the director of New York City's celebrated Hayden
Planetarium I get to decode the nature of the universe and create journeys through it for all the public to see.

What was not apparent, however, was the somewhat peculiar profile that I carried into the job. Although everyone's life
is unique, certain categories of life experience can be general-

ized: My tenure as a nerdy kid—complete with winnings in the science fair, membership in the physics club, and high scores in mathematics—greatly resembles all that you may have stereotyped for the world's community of nerds. My time as an athlete—as captain of my high school's wrestling team and as a varsity competitor in college—was no different from that of any other athlete. My interest in the universe—carrying me to the Ph.D. in astrophysics—led me down paths shared by many of my colleagues. And my life as a Black male in America—getting stopped for no reason by the police or being trailed by security guards in department stores—is hardly different from that of other Black males among my contemporaries. But when you combine all ingredients, my experiences offer a possibly unique portal through which to view life, society, and the universe.

More a rumination than a memoir, I wrote *The Sky Is Not the Limit* in a way that may reveal to the reader how scientists view the world—how I view the world. I want every generation of stargazers—whether they sit atop a tenement roof or an Appalachian mountain—to have a polished lens with which to see the universe and to reach for their own star.

# ONE

# NIGHT VISION

## BUILDING A RELATIONSHIP WITH THE SKY

### THE EARLY YEARS

IT WAS A DARK AND STARRY NIGHT. The sixty-five-degree air was calm. I felt as though I could see forever. Too numerous to count, the stars of the autumn sky, and the constellations they trace, were rising slowly in the east while the waxing crescent moon was descending into the western horizon. Aloft in the northern sky were the Big and Little Dippers, just where they were described to be, just as they were described to appear. The planets Jupiter and Saturn were high in the sky. One of the stars—I don't remember which—seemed to fall toward the horizon. It was a meteor streaking through the atmosphere. I was told there would be no clouds that night, but I saw one. It was long and skinny and stretched across the sky from hori-zon to horizon. No, I was mistaken. It wasn't a cloud. It was the Milky Way—with its varying bright and dark patches giving the appearance of structure and the illusion of depth. I had never seen the sky of the Milky Way with such clarity and majesty as that night.

Forty-five minutes of my suspended disbelief swiftly passed when the house lights came back on in the planetarium sky theater.

That was the night. The night the universe poured down from the sky and flowed into my body. I had been called. The study of the universe would be my career, and no force on Earth would stop me. I was just nine years old, but I now had an answer for that perennially annoying question all adults ask: "What do you want to be when you grow up?" Although I could barely pronounce the word, I would tell them, "I want to be an astrophysicist."

From that moment onward, one question lingered within me: Was this majestic planetarium sky an accurate portrayal of the real celestial sphere? Or was it a hoax? Surely there were too many stars. I had proof because I had seen the night sky from the Bronx—from the rooftop of my apartment house. Built upon one of the highest hills of the borough, it was one of a set of three buildings that were prophetically known as the Skyview Apartments.

In one of the other two Skyview buildings lived a close friend—a classmate in elementary school. My friend lived in a single-parent home with an older brother and sister, both of whom had active social agendas. The father, who retained custody of the three kids after the divorce, worked long hours and was only rarely at home. My friend, instead, spent a lot of time over at my place, especially on the weekends. His father assumed that the stability of my two-parent upbringing would add some structure and discipline to his life. While this may have been true, I am certain that my friend's influence on me was far greater. He taught me to play chess, poker, pinochle, Risk, and Monopoly. He introduced me to brainteaser books, which, if you are unfamiliar with the genre, are books that resemble collections of those dreaded word problems from your high school math class. Well-written brainteasers, however, have clever O. Henry–like plot twists in their answers that trick you with their simplicity. My favorite was: Start with four ants, one on each corner of a square board that measures twelve inches on a side. Each ant decides to walk at the same speed directly toward the ant to its right. By the time all four ants meet in the middle of the table, how far has each one traveled? (Answer: twelve inches.)

Or, start with a brand new, unshuffled deck of cards. The cards are sorted by suit and sequenced by number (typical of their configuration when first purchased). Cut the deck, just as one might do before a card game, but do it one hundred consecutive times. What are the chances that all fifty-two cards will still be sorted by suit *and* ordered by number? (Answer: 100 percent.)

I loved teasers that involved math: Counting one number per second, how long would it take to reach a trillion? (Answer: 31,710 years.) And more entertaining problems like: How many people must you collect into a room before you have a better-than-even chance that two of them would have the same birthday? (Answer: twenty-four.)

The more we played, the more stretched and sharpened my eleven-year-old brain became.

My friend's most important contribution to my life's path, however, was introducing me to binoculars. I had used them before—primarily to view sporting events and to look into other people's windows. My friend instead encouraged me to look up. He encouraged me to look beyond the streetlights, beyond the buildings, beyond the clouds, and out toward the Moon and stars of the night sky.

Nothing I can write will capture my acute cosmic imprinting when I first viewed the waxing crescent moon across the Hudson River and above the Palisades of New Jersey during a cloudless twilight evening. The Moon through those 7×35s was not just bigger, it was better. The coal-dark shadows sharply revealed its surface to be three-dimensional—a rich moonscape of mountains and valleys and craters and hills and plains. The Moon was no longer just a thing on the sky—it was another world in the universe. And if simple binoculars could transform the Moon, imagine what mountaintop telescopes could do with the rest of the universe.

Galileo was the first person in the world to look up with a good enough telescope to see what no one before him had ever dreamed: structure on the lunar surface, revolving spots on the Sun, the phases of Venus (just like the Moon), Saturn and its rings, Jupiter and its restless moons, and stars composing the faint glow of the Milky Way. When I too first saw these things I communed with Galileo across time and space. Galileo's "observatory" was his windowsill and his rooftop—so was mine. My discoveries, although old news for society, were no less astonishing for me than they must have been for Galileo in 1610.

I would soon learn to feed this intellectual hunger. My sixth-grade homeroom and science teacher was Mrs. Susan Kreindler, who was a tall woman with a keen sense of academic discipline. She was probably also one of the smartest teachers in my elementary school, PS-81. For the third quarter of my sixth grade report card she wrote, in round-hand cursive, "Less social involvement and more academic diligence is in order!"

Mrs. Kreindler also happens to be the teacher who, on her own time, clipped a small advertisement from the newspaper announcing that year's offering of astronomy courses at the Hayden Planetarium. One of them was called "Astronomy for Young People" and was for kids in junior high school and the first years of high school. Mrs. Kreindler knew of my growing interest in the universe, based on the proportion of astronomy-related book reports that I had been submitting. She concluded that the courses would probably not be out of my reach recommended that I explore them. She also figured that if my excess social energy were intelligently diverted outside the school, I could grow in ways unfettered by the formal limits of the classroom. Mrs. Kreindler packaged and redirected my "social involvement" that she had criticized. From then onward, the Hayden Planetarium became a much broader and deeper resource to the growth of my life's interests. I had previously known it only to be a place with a beautiful night sky—but I came to learn that the actual universe is much, much bigger.

A student's academic life experience can be constructed

from much more than what happens in a classroom. Good teachers know this. The best teachers make sure it happens.

The Skyview apartments, where I lived my formative years, are located in the northwest corner of the Bronx. All three buildings contained apartments lettered A through X in each of twenty-two stories. People tend to give residents of trailer parks a hard time for living in such small quarters. But apart from being bait for tornadoes, living in a trailer park can't be much different from being packed into New York City apartments. The buildings actually had twenty stories, not twenty-two, because the designers of most tall buildings in New York City (Skyview included) have succumbed to a bit of superstitious fear and omitted the thirteenth floor.

Suburban home dwellers normally assume they have little to envy of urban apartment dwellers, but I can think of at least one exception. During Halloween, the apartment dweller's bounty from trick-or-treating is without equal in all the suburbs of the land. My friends and I would each fill a large shopping bag of candy in less than forty-five minutes. We would acquire a full year's supply in an hour and a half. And since all roaming occurs indoors, you needn't remove your bedroom slippers to do it. Another advantage of apartment living comes from the height of the building's roof. An elevator ride to the top of the Bronx, with my telescope in tow, would give me an unobstructed view of the horizon at all points on the compass. As far as I knew, Mount Everest had nothing on me. But I had never been west of New Jersey.

When I was twelve, my family temporarily moved from the Bronx to Lexington, Massachusetts, an elite suburb of Boston. My father received a one-year appointment as a fellow at Harvard's Kennedy Institute of Politics, where he was also a research associate in the Program on Technology and Society. We sublet our New York apartment to live in a private home with a backyard, grass all around, a plum tree nearby, and a small brook out back. We lived on a small street called Peacock Farm Road. With a suburban address such as that, how could I ever face my city friends again?

That excursion to Lexington, my seventh grade in school, happened to be the most successful academic year of my life. I earned straight A's and won the school citizenship award (equivalent to that grade's valedictorian). Lots of people get straight A's—at least one per grade, often one per classroom. As adults, they tend to be collected and concentrated among the faculty of academia. The ascent to the Ph.D. continually sifts the mixture of students so that, at least in physics and astronomy, nearly every research scientist had a straight A average in high school or college or both.

My performance in seventh grade was nonetheless a personal achievement because I have never done so well in school, either before or since. I may never know for sure what ingredients made that year unique, but I watched no television and had no playgrounds in view of my bedroom window. There was also, of course, a spooky silence at night: no police sirens, no car horns, and no loud voices from people arguing on the street corner. Actually the nights weren't completely silent. I will not soon forget that annoying cacophony of crickets every evening. I have come to question why these sounds are considered "natural" while sounds made by members of our own species are considered "noise."

I did not grow accustomed to the crickets until I could extract environmental information from their behavior. I deduced for myself the semi-well-known relation between the rate of cricket sounds and the outdoor temperature: If you count the chirps in fifteen seconds, and then add forty, you get the temperature outside in Fahrenheit degrees. Only when the temperature dropped below forty degrees did the nights fall truly silent.

That year was also when I received my first telescope—a Christmas gift from my parents. My cosmic interests had already been established, so the 2.4-inch refractor with three eyepieces and a solar projection screen was not one of those "wishful thinking" gifts that parents are known to give their children. The telescope's educational value was immediate. And I had a backyard where I could observe the heavens for hours and hours without distractions of any kind. In the daytime I would observe the migration of sunspots move across the Sun's differentially rotating surface, tracking their twenty-five day journey. At night, with the relatively dark skies of suburban New England, the stars and planets were mine. During the snowy Massachusetts winters I would shovel a path to a circular clearing in our backyard so that I could observe even when everybody else was snowed in.

My love affair with the universe was in the fast lane, with my interests soon outstripping my telescope's power. All other things being equal, bigger telescopes are better than smaller telescopes. Unlike what you might be told in other sectors of life, when observing the universe, size does matter, which often leads to polite "telescope envy" at gatherings of amateur astronomers. Larger telescopes simply gather more light and see dimmer things. During my formative junior high school years back in New York, I received no weekly or monthly allowance from my parents, although they would not hesitate to buy affordable books on math and the universe that fed my interests. Expensive acquisitions required a job.

I bought my six-inch Newtonian reflecting telescope from monies earned by walking other people's dogs. These weren't ordinary dogs. These were apartment-dwelling city dogs, not to be confused with the streetwise variety that might live in an alley near the garbage dumpster. I walked large ones, small ones, mean ones, and friendly ones. But what they all had in common was disdain for inclement weather and a strong preference for taking the elevator over walking up or down the stairs. Going outside was a distraction from their warm and dry apartment life. Most dogs had raincoats. Some had hats and booties. I earned fifty cents per dog, per walk, during all my years in junior high school—enough to pay for two thirds of both my telescope and an entry-level Pentax SLR 35mm camera, equipped with specialized adapters for astrophotography. My parents kicked in the rest.

With its five-foot-long white tube, mounted with counterweights on a heavy-duty metal pier, my telescope looked like a cross between an artillery cannon and a grenade launcher. Like most telescopes above a certain cost, mine was equipped with an electric clock drive that compensated for Earth's rotation by tracking the motion of stars across the sky. The roof of my building had no power outlets, but my dentist (a lifelong friend of the family) happened to live on the nineteenth floor.

I would faithfully haul to the roof, along with my telescope, a hundred-foot heavy-duty extension cord and lower it into the bedroom window of his apartment. Actually, I often indentured my sister, four years my junior, to haul the heavy parts because I would not trust her with the lighter, but much more expensive, optical tube assembly.

In my mid-teen innocence, I was simply reaching out to the universe. As for nosy neighbors, my rooftop activities looked to them as though I were a heavily armed cat burglar, ready to rappel down the side of the apartment building in the dark, with my portable assault weapons strapped to my side. A third of the time I was on the roof, someone would call the police.

Whatever has been said of police officers, I have yet to meet one who was not impressed by the sight of the Moon, planets, or stars through a telescope. Saturn alone bailed me out a half-dozen times. For all I know, I would have been shot to death on numerous occasions were it not for the majesty of the night sky.

During my junior high school and high school years, I took at least a half-dozen courses offered by instructors on staff at the Hayden Planetarium. The subject levels and the expertise of the instructors merged with my stage of learning to create the most influential set of courses in my life.

Among the instructors, if there were ever a "Voice of God" contest, Dr. Fred Hess would win. Dr. Hess is a friendly man with the body proportions of Santa Claus and a public trustworthiness rivaling that of Walter Cronkite. I took two courses from him inside the Sky Theater of the Hayden Planetarium. One of them was titled "Stars, Constellations, and Legends." The resonant frequencies of his amplified voice within the hemispherical cavity of the Planetarium dome somehow conspired to create a fatherly, yet godlike, sound that emanated from the depths of space. At a time when I was beginning to take advanced math and physics classes, Hess's course reveled in the majesty and romance of the night sky, and reaffirmed for me the simple joys of just looking up.

My current lecture manner and style under the dome of the Sky Theater, and under the canopy of the night sky itself, remain traceable to the talents of Dr. Hess. He also happens to be a seasoned eclipse chaser and is among the top few people in the world for total logged time in the Moon's shadow.

For most of the years I attended these Hayden courses, the chairman of the Planetarium was Dr. Mark Chartrand III. After a long string of athletic heroes, from track stars to baseball players, I finally met someone who would break the athletic mold and serve as my first intellectual role model. I didn't want to be him, I simply wanted to know the universe the way he knew the universe. Dr. Chartrand possessed a combination of pedagogical enthusiasm, a command of astrophysics, and a sense of humor that I had never dreamed was possible. I took two courses from him over the years. My favorite between them, and my favorite of them all, was simply titled "Special Topics in Astrophysics," which covered the physics and the mathematics of relativity, black holes, quasars, and the big bang. At age fifteen, I was the youngest in the class by at least fifteen years, but I had to begin somewhere if I was ever going to have the cosmos at my fingertips. Dr. Chartrand became the strongest intellectual influence on my teenage years.

Of all the planets in the sky, my favorite is Saturn. Without question, debate, or argument, Saturn is the most beautiful. Saturn was also the first planet that I ever saw through my first telescope. Imagine the thrill of first locating a point of light on the sky. Then centering it in the crosshairs of a finder scope and looking through the telescope's eyepiece to reveal another world—a celestial orb surrounded by a ring system three times the width of the planet itself. Several moons are clearly visible through a simple telescope, but at last count twenty or so are catalogued.

One of the projects in my seventh grade woodworking shop was to make a lamp. I decided to craft one of my own design even though the class was encouraged to use several pre-designed styles. One lamp style was inspired by a water pump—you press down the pump handle to turn the lamp on and off. Another was a mini wine keg, where the lightbulb was where the stopper would go and the switch was the spigot. These designs were clever and tested key shop skills, but none resonated within me. My wooden lamp would have a cosmic theme. My wooden lamp would be designed after a planet. My wooden lamp would be Saturn. In my design the lightbulb housing emerged from the top of a lathed, white pine sphere about nine inches in diameter. Two dowels emerged from the equator of the ball to support a broad ma-hogany ring that tilted on the dowels. With the lamp's chain connected from the base of the bulb housing to the ring's edge, the lamp could be turned on and off by tilting Saturn's ring. A wooden pedestal ball supported the ball from below, with a layer of felt underneath to protect the furniture upon which it rested.

I got an A+, and it remains my primary desk lamp today.

I enjoyed another encounter with Saturn while on board the SS *Canberra* on the way back from viewing the total solar eclipse of June 30, 1973* off the coast of northwest Africa. With a mobile platform, you are no longer susceptible to inclement or otherwise cloudy weather on the day of the eclipse, provided you carry along a reliable meteorologist. This particular Cunard luxury liner had been converted to a floating scientific laboratory where all manner of astrophysical experiments were conducted during the seven minutes of blocked sunlight—one of the longest eclipses on record. (A decade later, the ship would be converted once again, but this time into a military transport to ferry British troops to the southern hemisphere during the Falkland Islands war.) I had received a small scholarship from the Explorers Club of New York to take this trip alone. At age fourteen, I was the youngest unaccompanied person on the boat, but I had my telescope in tow, which was all the guardianship I needed. And when people asked me my age, I lied and told them that I was sixteen.

Two thousand scientists, engineers, and eclipse enthusiasts were on board, as well as assorted luminaries such as the astronauts Neil Armstrong and Scott Carpenter. The prolific Dr. Isaac

---

*July 1973 coincided with the 500th anniversary of the birth of the Polish astronomer Nicolaus Copernicus, the father of the sun-centered model of the Universe.

Asimov was also on board. He gave a thoroughly entertaining and informative lecture (steeped in his inimitable Brooklyn accent), on the history of eclipses. This was the first and only occasion I have met him. (But fifteen years later, I would remind Dr. Asimov about this eclipse cruise in a letter, humbly requesting that he write a jacket blurb for my first book, *Merlin's Tour of the Universe*. He agreed.) The Hayden Planetarium was represented by four scientists and educators, including Dr. Fred Hess and Dr. Mark Chartrand III, who were repeatedly featured as lecturers during the cruise.

There we were, off the coast of northwest Africa, and the two leading educators on the ship worked at New York City's Hayden Planetarium. I was a lucky guy.

In addition to the multiple dozens of educational lectures and presentations, the journey home included fun intellectual diversions such as an astronomy trivia contest, where my knowledge of Saturn happened to matter greatly. With about fifty contestants, teamed in tables of four or five, a master of ceremonies started asking all manner of questions about the cosmos. Successions of hard questions swiftly eliminated many tables. One question stumped everyone: "Which day of the year can never have a total solar eclipse?" I was thinking about dates of the year when I should have been thinking about days of the year. The correct answer was Easter, which is defined to fall on the first Sunday after the first full moon after the first day of spring in the Northern Hemisphere. Easter therefore falls, at most, seven days after the full moon, while total solar eclipses can happen only during the moment of the new moon, which falls a full two weeks away from the full moon. I grew to learn that practically any moon-based holiday that did not specify the astronomical new moon would also qualify as a correct answer, such as Good Friday, Passover, Ramadan, and the Chinese New Year.

Another question that stumped and therefore eliminated a bunch of tables was "What are the linguistically correct names for objects or aliens from Mars, Venus, and Jupiter?" I knew this one cold. While everybody knew that aliens from Mars are called Martians, fewer people knew that aliens from Jupiter are called Jovians. And only a handful of people knew that aliens from Venus are called Venereals. The word "Venereal" is not in common use among astronomers, in favor of the less contagious-sounding "Venutian." Blame the medical community, which snatched the word long before astronomers had any good use for it. Venus is the goddess of love and beauty, so I suppose she ought to be the goddess of its medical consequences.

At the end of the contest, two tables remained in the running, including mine. The final question was "What feature of Saturn, other than its beautiful ring system, strongly distinguishes it from all other planets in the solar system?" I knew that my Saturn lamp (from seventh grade shop class) would float if you tossed it into a bathtub because it was made of wood and wood is less dense than water. So too would the planet Saturn float if you could find a bathtub big enough to place it. Saturn is the only planet whose average density is less than that of water. I stood up before the assemblage and delivered the winning answer. For that bit of trivia I earned applause from everyone in the room and a free bottle of champagne for my table. Having gazed so long at the stars, I now had my first taste of being one—if only for a brief but sparkling moment.

My second real trip away from my family was during the August that followed my ninth grade in junior high school. Destination: Camp Uraniborg, an outpost in the Mojave Desert of Southern California directed by Mr. Rick Schaefer and Mr. Joseph Patterson for kids whose parents didn't know what else to do with their precocious progeny for the summer. Uraniborg was the name of the Danish astronomer Tycho Brahe's six-teenth-century telescopeless observatory, where, using preci-sion sighting instruments, he made seminal observations of the positions of planets as they moved against the background stars.

Whatever could have possessed two rational adults to lease land in the desert, acquire a dozen high-performance tele-scopes, assemble a teaching staff of mathematicians, physicists, and astronomers, and invite early teenage astronomy buffs to spend a month living nocturnally? I don't really know, but Schaefer and Patterson created something special indeed. They created it out of a deep love for astronomy and an even deeper love for teaching it to others.

To get there, I joined a half-filled van of others from the East Coast and we were driven for fifty-three consecutive hours from New York City to the secluded campsite, thirty miles be-yond Barstow, California. For a month I lived nocturnally, gained access to a bank of high-performance telescopes, pro-grammed a computer, and took courses in math, relativity, op-tics, and astrophysics.

I thought I had died and gone to the great sky beyond.

From New York City, on a good night, you might see a hundred stars. That night from the Mojave Desert I saw bezillions. Apparently my first sky show, six years earlier, was not a hoax after all. Near-zero humidity. Dark, cloudless skies. I couldn't help thinking to myself, "It reminds me of the Hayden Planetarium sky," which is an embarrassingly urban thought. That summer I obtained the greatest color photographs I have ever taken of the night sky—before or since. The portfolio includes moons, planets, star systems, galaxies, nebulae, and large swaths of our own Milky Way galaxy. I had captured the soul of the night sky with my Pentax SLR camera on Kodak's High Speed Ektachrome film.

During the daytime hours, I used Kodachrome to capture the desert desolance. For astrophotography at night, however, the High Speed Ektachrome was the most light-sensitive color film then commercially available—ideal for the astronomer on the go.

Kodachrome film happened to inspire a song of the same title by Paul Simon, which was receiving considerable airtime on the radio that summer. During the cross-country caravan to Camp Uraniborg, a pop-music radio station somewhere in the Midwest bleeped the word "crap" from "Kodachrome"'s opening line: "When I think back on all the *crap* I learned in High School . . ."

Where the %@!# was I?

Wasn't this supposed to be America? Land of liberty and the freedom of speech? At age fourteen I had never noticed that while our nation is indeed a union, and while we have an interstate highway connecting us all, it's possible for one state to be socially, politically, and philosophically disconnected from the next. Fortunately, the laws of physics apply everywhere on Earth and in the heavens and are independent of social mores. These same laws were beginning to serve as one of my intellectual anchors amid the irrationalities of society.

No less memorable than snuggling with the cosmos that summer was snuggling with the palette of insects and other creatures that claim the desert as their home. The only scorpion I had ever seen was the one of my imagination, traced by the stars of the zodiacal constellation Scorpius. That summer I was shaking them out of my boots each morning—boots I was wearing to protect my ankles from star-bathing rattlesnakes at night.

Whoever said the desert is a tranquil place? Unlike urban lunatics, Mojave desert coyotes don't need the sight of a celestial orb as an excuse for their unruly behavior—they howled every night, Moon or no Moon. And there is no doubt about it; bulbous, hairy tarantulas are much uglier, and far more terrifying, than any other creature in the solar system.

After a week's exposure to desert bug fauna, I started longing for the simplicity of urban household cockroaches. They don't sting, bite, suck blood, or inject venom. And they generally stay out of your way.

Camp Uraniborg no longer exists, but the influence upon its participants was indelible. Five(!) of my fellow campers from Uraniborg went on for Ph.D.s in astrophysics, and we all overlapped at one time or another in graduate school. Joe Patterson later went on for his Ph.D. in astronomy at the University of Texas and is now a full professor of astronomy at Columbia University in New York City. He has also served as a latter-day mentor for me during the transfer of my graduate program from Texas to Columbia.

My experience at Camp Uraniborg remains one of the most enduring and influential episodes of my life. I was on a path that first came into view the moment my eleven-year-old eyes viewed the Moon through my friend's binoculars. My earliest memories of life begin at age four, watching an episode of *The Mickey Mouse Club* on television with my older brother and mother, who was pregnant with my sister. By age fourteen (my age at Camp Uraniborg) my interests in the universe had already occupied a third of my sentient years.

By summer's end of 1973, my fate was set. I had just returned from my one-month session at Camp Uraniborg, where I had obtained striking photographs of cosmic objects. I had acquired my second telescope and I was a card-carrying member of New York's Amateur Astronomers Association. Meanwhile, news had broken that the Czech astronomer Lubos Kohoutek had found a beautiful new comet in the sky. It was discovered much farther out in the solar system than where new comets are typically found, which was a sure indication that its brightness would increase to record levels as it neared the Sun that December.

Comets are basically big balls of dusty ice up to a few dozen miles in diameter. They all orbit in elongated paths around the Sun and represent debris from the formation of the planets nearly five billion years ago. As comets near the Sun's radiant energy, their surface ice changes directly from solid to gas, just as does dry ice—frozen $CO_2$—on Earth. The evaporated dust and gases collect around the comet's nucleus, forming an enormous spherical envelope called a coma that can reach millions of miles in diameter. The dust and gases also stream forth into interplanetary space and form a "tail" that gets pushed away from the nucleus by sunlight and the solar wind. The tail can extend up to a hundred million miles but will always point opposite to the direction of the Sun, no matter which direction the comet happens to be moving. That winter, Comet Kohoutek would be easily visible to the unaided eye and was the most anticipated comet in a generation.

During the months that immediately preceded the comet's closest approach to the Sun, I began to see anxiety-ridden people on the street urging others toward repentance. They claimed that the new comet was a sign that the end of the world was near. I wondered how this scene was possible. Only a few years earlier, Apollo astronauts were bounding about on the Moon. To my growing sense of reason, full-grown adults couldn't possibly be so ignorant of simple scientific truths. Actually, there is no shame in not knowing. The problem arises when irrational thought and attendant behavior fill the vacuum left by ignorance. I had been learning that throughout history, the arrival of comets, the appearance of planetary alignments, and the spectacle of eclipses consistently extracted irrational behavior in people. For example, the appearance of Comet Halley in A.D. 1066 was blamed almost entirely for the Norman conquest of England in the same year. Okay. That was a millennium ago. I just couldn't imagine the prevalence of such behavior in modern times. Maybe that missing thirteenth floor of my apartment building signaled a still deeper condition in society. Perhaps I could no longer revel in the beauty of the universe without accepting the tandem duty of sharing its laws and operations with those whose superstitions leave them in fear of it.

As word of Comet Kohoutek spread through the land, word of my cosmic interests spread among my extended relatives and family friends. The family network helped in many and varied ways to provide an intellectual buoyancy to my pursuits. One of my mother's cousins worked in the Brooklyn Public Library and never failed to send de-accessioned astronomy and math books my way. A close friend of my parents had some expertise in photography and black-and-white film processing. She served as a first mentor in my early days of astrophotography. Another close friend of the family, who happened to be professor of education at the City College of New York, recommended me to one of her colleagues who was an instructor at CCNY's Workshop Center for Open Education—a program offering contined education programs for adults. The instructor, in turn, invited me to give a talk to her fall classes on whatever topics or aspects of the universe interested me. The coming of Comet Kohoutek was by then a weekly news item. With my astrophotographs freshly taken through the lenses and mirrors of desert telescopes and Kohoutek to talk about, I gladly accepted the invitation.

To a class of about fifty people, I devoted most of an hour to describing the subjects of my photo-essay—from planets to stars to the Milky Way galaxy, ending with a special discussion of the lore and science of comets and what the winter sky would look like with Comet Kohoutek as a visitor. I wasn't nervous, even though the room was filled with people who were two, three, and four times my age. For me, talking about the universe was like breathing. I suppose it was no different from another kid talking about his treasured baseball card collection, or a film buff recalling scenes from a favorite movie. I could not have been more comfortable sharing what I knew.

Three days later I received a check in the mail for $50, with a request to return and give two more lectures. Apparently this was their standard compensation for visiting speakers. At the time, the minimum wage was somewhere around $3.00 per hour and I was a few weeks past my fifteenth birthday. Given these two facts, $50 looked like a semi-infinite amount of money for an hour's work. In dog-walking units, that's one hundred walks.

After I landed back on Earth, I confess that I felt a little like an information prostitute. I had never before been paid to speak—paid to share information that I just happened to have lying around in my head. Could the act of helping or enlightening others be classified as remunerable labor? Imagine volunteering to help a little old lady across the street, and when you get to the other side she pays you for your efforts. You didn't do it for the money. You did it because it was the right thing to do and because it felt good. How dare the instructor even make the offer. Of course, I didn't return the check. My fleeting feelings of financial morality were replaced with the lesson that knowledge and intelligence were no less a commodity than sweat and blood.

That December, when Kohoutek was at its brightest, the comet was barely noticeable to the unaided eye. Most people had to be told where to look. It was simply a dud. The scientific community would learn for the first time that comets with orbits lasting hundreds of thousands to millions of years (like that of Kohoutek) tend to evaporate inefficiently, and as a re-sult, produce tiny comas and tails. Fortunately, I was not asked to return the $50.

The following summer, I went on a two-week trip to the out-skirts of a very small town called Kilmartin in northern Scotland with an outfit called Educational Expeditions International. There I joined a team of scientists and surveyors to excavate and map the astronomical alignments of uncharted prehistoric megaliths, not unlike those of Stonehenge. The monies came from a grant by the United States Department of Education, Office of the Gifted and Talented. After several levels of com-petition, from local, through city, and then state, I was be-knighted "Gifted and Talented," a designation I resented then and now. Who were my talents a gift from? Hadn't I worked hard and long to achieve my expertise? The title specifically omits people who fall below the arbitrary "gifted" threshold. A more appropriate, though less catchy, title might be the Department of Education's "Office of the Students who Work Hard." Such a title would, instead, challenge the nonwinners to do better next time rather than to give up.

After a fortnight of surveying and analysis of the astronomical abilities of prehistoric civilizations of the British Isles, I was on my way back home. As I passed through London's Heathrow Airport I spotted a newspaper whose banner headline announced that President Nixon had resigned over the Watergate hotel break-ins. I was immediately thrust back into the real world, although I pre-ferred to think that it was the universe and not Watergate that rep-resents the real world.

These various travel opportunities did not just drop out of the sky. My awareness of them along with partial financial support are traceable to a single individual, Mr. Vernon Grey, the director of education of New York City's Explorers Club. We met in Dr. Chartrand's "Special Topics in Astrophysics" course. After I had asked a bunch of questions during one of the classes, Mr. Grey walked up to me in a quiet and unassuming manner. He introduced himself, handed me his business card, and invited me to call him when I had the chance. Not yet business card–savvy, I did not even read what the card said, but I put it in my wallet and said thank you.

When I got home later than evening, I showed the business card to my mother, who immediately knew the ramifications. She called him the next day and learned that the Explorers Club had reference databases and scholarship programs for budding scientists to attend expeditions all around the world.

How often I wonder how different my life would have been, what different paths I would have taken, had I not taken the Hayden course that led to my encounter with Mr. Grey.

Come senior year of high school I was captain of the wrestling team. But I was also editor in chief of the 1976 *Physical Science Journal*, which ranks, along with the editors in chief of the annual *Math Bulletin* and *Biology Journal*, as the most prestigious title one can hold in the school. I was proud of that volume. It featured my field report from Scotland, as well as a dozen other original research articles from my classmates. Titles included "Non-linear Stensor Analysis," "Using Hafnium-182 to Treat Malignant Melanoma of the Conjunctivae," and

"The Determination of the Technological Feasibility of the Photon Rocket." The cover page portrayed the plaque that had been affixed to the side of *Pioneer 10*, the first space probe to have enough energy to leave the solar system and enter interstellar space. The plaque displays a line drawing of a nude man and woman along with a host of symbols and signs intended to give intelligent aliens our location in space along with the inside scoop on our scientific discoveries. The last page contained an assortment of physics brainteasers while all pages used the sequence of element symbols from the Periodic Table to designate page numbers.

At sixty-four pages, that edition of the *Journal* was, at the time, the largest ever produced at the school in any subject.

In the fall of my senior year, I applied to five colleges, including Harvard, MIT, and Cornell, which were my top three choices. As a courtesy to applicants, the Ivy League schools (plus MIT) notify you by midwinter about whether your application is unlikely, possible, or likely to gain you admission to the school. The first of these to arrive was from MIT, on a day when I just happened to be retrieving the mail. While standing in front of my open mailbox, I held the envelope up to the sunlight, which was piercing the mailroom's window (as though if I had opened the envelope quickly, the result would magically be changed for the worse). That's when I glimpsed the word "Likely," circled boldly in red, and that's when I knew the next chapter in my life was set. That moment represented the greatest emotional swing I have ever experienced—from a state of high anxiety in one instant, to a prostrate and teary-eyed state the next.

For most of my high school years, I subscribed to the

*Scientific American.* The "About the Authors" section was my favorite, for it contained all sorts of personal information about the contributing scientists, such as where they went to school and what their side interests were. One prominent astrophysicist had also been National Greco-Roman wrestling champion. When it came to actually choosing a college to attend, I devised a decision matrix that tallied the number of physics and astronomy articles in *Scientific American* written by scientists who had been undergraduates at the schools that admitted me. I also tallied where these same authors earned their master's degrees, their Ph.D.s, and where they were currently on the faculty. Harvard won in every category, although Cornell represented a strong draw for me because of Professor Carl Sagan.

I first met Carl (as he preferred to be called) when I visited Cornell for the required interview. My letter of application had been dripping with an interest in the universe. The admissions office, unbeknown to me, forwarded the application to Carl Sagan's attention. Within weeks I received a personal letter inviting me up to Ithaca to visit him. Was this, I asked myself, the same Carl Sagan that I had seen on Johnny Carson? Was this the same Carl Sagan that had written all those books on the universe? Indeed it was. I visited him on a snowy afternoon in February (I later learned that many winter afternoons in Ithaca are snowy). Carl was warm, compassionate, and demonstrated what appeared to be a genuine interest in my life's path. At the end of the day, he drove me back to the Ithaca bus station and jotted down his home phone number—just in case the bus could not navigate through the snow and I needed a place to stay.

I never told him this, but at every stage of my scientific career that followed, I have modeled my encounters with students after my first encounter with Carl.

I did not ultimately attend Cornell University, because the data from my matrix analysis of *Scientific American* authors was too compelling to forgo. I was off to Harvard, but not before my manhood would be tested.

As spring began, during my senior year of high school, New York City received one of those winter's-last-stand snowfalls that dropped four or five inches. School wasn't canceled but it might as well have been. Most seniors, myself included, took very long recesses (i.e., we cut classes) to engage in a school-wide snowball fight. Off to the side of the fight, leaning against their motorcycles, were several students who were never seen without their black leather jackets. They were the "greasers" and represented the toughest faction of the school. I cannot judge how tough they were on an absolute scale, but on the Bronx Science scale, they were the meanest things on two feet. During the snowball fight, the greasers that day were noncombatants, but one of my high-arching snowballs happened to veer off course, like a sliced golf shot, and hit squarely on the chest of the most feared greaser. As the snowball exploded on his body, it scattered snow into his face with his girlfriend in full view, tucked under his arm.

A most unfortunate incident.

Anybody with less testosterone would just have laughed it off. But this greaser immediately yelled all manner of expletives and racial epithets across the yard to me, with fist clenched and waving in the air. While sound does not travel well across fields of snow, I heard him clearly say that I had better not walk past him and return to school that afternoon, under threat of bodily harm.

An hour later, at the end of the snowball fight, most people were cold, wet, and tired. The perfect occasion to return to class. As I slowly approached the school, in defiance of his previous commandments, the angry greaser started walking toward the main door at a pace that would perfectly intersect my arrival. When I walked, instead, to the side door, he slightly quickened his pace to greet me there. As we came within about ten feet of each other, he drew his "007" pocketknife, which has a six-inch locking blade with a wooden handle and can be opened as swiftly as a spring-loaded stiletto. We had stopped within two feet of each other when he placed himself between me and the school door. We had never before stood so close to each other. I think he was slightly surprised that I was two inches taller, even after you accounted for the one-inch heels of his motorcycle boots. He may also have been surprised that while I mildly tried to avoid him, upon reentering the school, I did not flinch, nor did I show any sign of fear when we stood face-to-face.

He wielded the knife in the sunlight, with its reflection beaming across my face. I thought this sort of thing happened only in the movies. Holding his knife within a foot of my face, his first words were, "You hit my leather jacket with a snowball." I next compressed what would normally be fifteen minutes of logical reasoning into what was probably only two or three seconds of my silence. My timed mental flow chart went something like this:

T = 0 seconds

> *He wants to engage me in a fight.*
>
> *He has a large sharp knife and I don't.*
>
> *I am captain of the wrestling team and I am bigger than he is.*
>
> *I am probably also quicker, and I have some training in martial arts.*
>
> *I could probably disarm him and pin him to the ground.*
>
> *But then he would lose the fight and be angrier still.*

T = 1 second

> *He and his friends would surely seek revenge before year's end.*
>
> *I would live my final months of high school in fear and terror.*
>
> *Suppose I failed to disarm him?*
>
> *However small that chance is, I would be cut badly and possibly die.*
>
> *I have much more to lose in this fight than he has to gain.*
>
> *I am already accepted at Harvard, the college of my choice.*
>
> *My entire life of astrophysics is ahead of me.*

T = 2 seconds

> *My identity is not built on my ego nor my machismo.*
>
> *After all, it was my snowball that hit him.*

*Mahatma Gandhi and Martin Luther King Jr.*
   *praised nonviolence.*
*If I humbly refuse to engage, he has no force to*
   *combat.*
*With no force to combat, he may just disarm him-*
   *self.*

T = 3 seconds

   Like the one-line output of a long computer program, my mouth promptly uttered the following
   sentence: *"I am sorry I hit you with a snowball. It*
   *was unintentional and will not happen again."*

We stared at each other in silence for several seconds more
before he folded up his knife, returned it to his pocket, and
walked back to his motorcycle. I quietly passed through the
door and returned to class, having retained my health, my dignity, and my future.

## THE MIDDLE YEARS

Much has been written about the value of a broad formal education to one's enlightenment. But when all is learned, a double standard remains. At cocktail parties, if a conversation
touches upon late nineteenth century literature, or baroque
music, or Renaissance art, then the participants are tagged as
"erudite." But if the conversation is about the hadron super-
collider or about the hydrodynamics of dams, the participants
are tagged as "geeks." Nobody ever passes judgment on those
who admit, "I was never any good at math." Such statements

are just accepted. But have a look at people's reactions if someone were to confess, "I was never any good at nouns and
verbs." I am occasionally (though playfully) chastised for not
knowing some character or another from a Shakespeare play,
or from the President's cabinet. Yet, in spite of these double
standards, I have come to realize that whatever I know that
isn't science, I know far more of it than the science known by
others.

At the Bronx High School of Science, the environment bred
logical and analytical minds, so I had not imagined that a liberal arts component to my formal education would amount to
anything more than an academic curiosity. I have since bene-
fited greatly from my nonscience training, especially in college, where more than half my coursework fell outside my
field of concentration. It all started my freshman year, when I
took a course titled "Humanities 15." In this full-year survey
of art and design, I didn't just learn about art and design, I actually did it.

And I have never been the same.

The course was offered in one of the studios of Harvard's
Carpenter Center for Visual Arts, a hypermodern building designed by Le Corbusier—his only building in the Western
Hemisphere. The professor of the course was Lou Banawski, one
of the founding partners of the Cambridge Seven, a well-known
design firm in Cambridge, Massachusetts. All the ingredients were
in place, and I was in the belly of the beast.

Charcoal drawing led off the syllabus at the beginning of
September. The instructor first played recorded music of various genres and asked us to draw the music's energy. Excuse
me. You want me to do what? Energy is $mc^2$ or $\frac{1}{2}mv^2$ or $mgh$

or $G\dfrac{m_1 m_2}{r}$. Energy is *not* something you draw while hearing music. One of the hallmarks of science is its precision of language and concepts. What else could I think of the assignment but that it was a waste of my time, tuition money, and of course, energy.

By mid September we were drawing nudes, which interested me much more than drawing music—although I think the human body is overrated as a thing of beauty, especially when compared with truly heavenly bodies. By the end of September, we were drawing miscellaneous objects piled in the front of the studio—rocking chairs, drapes, balls, trunks—stuff you might find in somebody's attic.

When October arrived, we were drawing a heap of funky-looking pumpkins. By month's end, I must have drawn a thousand of them. I was fluid. I was focused. I was dreaming pumpkins in my sleep. In fact, I'd bet I can draw pumpkins better than anybody else in the universe. All was well in "Humanities 15" until the instructor commanded, "No longer draw the pumpkins. Draw the space between the pumpkins."

My logical mind promptly snapped.

After a month of pumpkin worship, these things all of a sudden became boundaries to the absence of pumpkin, in which I was to endow the same level of meaning and existence that I had previously granted the pumpkins themselves. To the instructor, I must have looked like what dogs look like when you play a high-pitched sound and they tilt their head with quizzical curiosity.

I eventually became pretty good at drawing the nothing between the something, and I would never look upon the human universe the same way. My private world transformed overnight, from one occupied by all things chemical and physical to one occupied by the juxtaposition of shapes and forms. I broke free from a logic box that I did not know had contained me. From then onward I welcomed all manner of verbal abstractions and creative use of vocabulary into my life. From it I continue to derive insights into art, literature, music, and the human condition. I encourage the liberal artists of the world to take a conjugate excursion through the land of logic. For one to thrive in the real world probably requires mastery of both.

My entering class at Harvard contained your usual list of children of luminaries, with Caroline Kennedy and her late cousin Michael Kennedy leading the list. The Harvard student body is steeped in social traditions that derive from the power of wealth and political influence. The father of a good friend in my dorms was the governor of Puerto Rico. The father of the wrestling team captain my sophomore year was the Speaker of the House of Representatives.

But I was indifferent to it all.

Many, perhaps most, people who attend Harvard do so to share in these Ivy League legacies. I was simply there as my next step in becoming a scientist, and not much else mattered. Not the football games, the student protests, nor the social rituals. And yes, I confess to actually saying, "Not Yo-Yo Ma again" the fourth or fifth time he gave a cello recital in one of my dorm's common rooms during his senior year.

One of the few lasting elements of Harvard's traditions on my life appears as a double inscription over one of the arches to the Harvard Yard, where I lived as a freshman. As you pass under the arch from the street, the inscription reads "Enter to grow in wisdom." Three years later I would discover its companion inscription, immediately on the other side of the arch and visible as you leave the yard: "Exit to Serve Better Thy Country and Thy Kind."

My list of life's most influential mentors continued to grow. In graduate school at the University of Texas at Austin, where I earned my master's degree in astronomy, I was a teaching assistant for nearly all the semesters I was enrolled. Three needs were served by this arrangement: I became eligible for in-state tuition, the department got much needed help in managing and running its battery of labs and introductory astronomy courses (UT has one of the largest programs in the nation), and I acquired teaching tips from the professors.

Not many professors in this world actually care whether the lecture they deliver is the same as the lecture received by the attending students. For the two to be the same requires a certain level of sensitivity to how student minds can misinterpret what you tell them. My own teaching methods were honed and refined after working for Professor Frank N. Bash. He remains the only professor I have ever seen who teaches to the mind of the student and not to the syllabus or the chalkboard. He eschewed multiple-choice exams, which of course significantly increased my burden as a grader, and promoted the verbal logic inherent in well-posed scientific problems. By the end of every introductory astronomy course that he taught, the students knew how to think about the physical world around them. Other than Bash's course, I know of no other in all of academia where students who got C's would still claim that the course was the best they have ever taken. I am a better teacher, a better professor, and a better educator for my time spent as a T.A. under Professor Bash. At the moment, he and I both happen to serve on the Board of Directors of the American Astronomical Society, the professional organization of the nation's astrophysicists.

On the graduate research side of the academic fence, one of several advisers on my master's thesis at the University of Texas was the late professor Gerard de Vaucouleurs, one of the last of the old-world scientists. He knew Russian, German, French, and a little bit of Latin, all of which gave him access to the historical, untranslated scientific literature. He had an encyclopedic knowledge of all published research relevant to his own. And he was the most meticulous scientist I have ever known. He logged four or five comments, suggestions, and criticisms per page on the 130-page draft of my master's thesis. Other committee members logged four or five notes per chapter. More than anyone else, de Vaucouleurs has instilled within me an uncommon sense of patience, precision, and scientific fortitude. No idea is too big to tackle. And no detail is too small to spend days or weeks investigating. Like the Stradivarius violin, I fear that his kind will never again be made.

I also attended a course taught by Professor John Archibald Wheeler, who is generally credited with inventing the term "black hole," where a blob of matter has collapsed upon itself, closing off the surrounding fabric of space and time from the rest of the universe. A former student of Albert Einstein's, Professor Wheeler, in all his brilliance, remains humble in the presence of the majesty of physical law. As if the laws of nature were a fence that we all must ascend. We stand together on the same side of this fence, taking measure of how high the fence is and how hard it is to climb. Wheeler is also humble about what he knows and honest about what he does not know. He is therefore quick to admit an error. He always carried a supply of pennies in his pocket when he taught his graduate physics classes. If you caught him making a mistake on the chalkboard he would stop the class and publicly hand you one of these pennies. These are deep yet simple traits by which we all should live, but they are especially rare among leading scientists.

I also happened to meet my wife-to-be in his relativity class.

My take-home stipend as a teaching assistant was about $6,000 per year, and my rent was $400 per month for a very small one-bedroom apartment, which left about $3.00 per day on which to live. With a budget such as this, one's food choices at the supermarket become somewhat limited. Assorted combinations of pasta, rice, beans, pork neck bones, eggs, canned tuna, bread, and cheese can get you far. But I remained athletically active after college and my demand for calories outstripped my capacity to feed myself on $3.00 per day. For the first time in my life, I was unintentionally losing weight.

I needed another source of income.

I don't know why, but the first thought to come to mind was to become a male stripper at a nearby women-only nightclub. The place was only a half mile away, between where I lived and downtown Austin. I was relatively flexible and graceful for my size (6 feet 2 inches, 190 pounds), having been a performing member of two dance companies while in college, and I was in pretty good shape, having wrestled Division I varsity in the NCAA. I could do easy flexible things like sit in a full lotus position, and while standing with straightened legs, bend over and palm the ground with both hands. Commensurate with my training, however, I could also execute harder moves, like a side to side leg split; I could put my foot behind my head while seated; I could grab my instep and raise either of my legs straight up over my head while standing; and I could curl backward from a standing position until the back of my head touched my heels.

I figured I could work at the club for just one or two nights per week to make enough money.

Of all the (legal) ways to earn fast cash, including giving blood or making donations to the sperm bank, the nightclub concept intrigued me most. I finally assembled the courage to observe one evening's worth of dance sets. In addition to one's own choreography, several group numbers were mainstays of the club. One of them, the finale with all dancers, required that you wear only a jockstrap. But these were not ordinary jockstraps; they were specially designed with asbestos lining and they were soaked with lighter fluid. Upon igniting them—yes, igniting them—the dancers sprang onto the stage shaking their buns and their flaming privy housings to the 1958 Jerry Lee Lewis hit "Great Balls of Fire."

I thought calmly to myself, "How desperate am I?"

I am embarrassed to say that only at that moment did the obvious occur to me: Maybe I should be a math tutor. To set one's genitals on fire seemed less like the need to dance than the absence of a creative solution to my money problems.

And so it came to pass that I tutored undergraduates in math and physics, through a campus organization that ensured a continuous supply of students in need of help, and a continuous supply of money. You just never know when and where you might need the math you were taught in school.

I should have known well in advance of my strip club excursion that tutoring was the way to go. The only time I ever attended a maximum security prison was while in college as a volunteer math tutor for prisoners seeking their Graduate Equivalency Diploma. The prison was Walpole State Penitentiary near Walpole, Massachussets. Cell Block Ten was death row, where an electric chair was housed. My student prisoner was a breaking-and-entering specialist. His name was Carlos, and he showed me the scars from several bullet holes the local police put in his body before he was apprehended on his last convenience store robbery. He had done okay on the reading sections of the GED exam but his math skills were poor. He needed help with fractions and their arithmetic manipulations. These weekly visits forever changed my view of prisons and prisoners.

After walking through a metal detector that was sensitive enough to be triggered by a shoemaker's nails in the heels of your shoes, you pass through a set of double steel doors embedded in a reinforced concrete wall. The passage through the wall remains in sight from a downward-looking guard tower that affords a view through a wide hole in the passageway's ceiling. The prison guards all wore miniature handcuffs as tie clips. Prisoners convicted of sex crimes were not particularly safe on the main floor of the prison. There was an implicit hierarchy of crimes for which you would earn either the respect or the ire of other inmates. In this subsociety of castoffs there was no crime more noble than killing your wife or girlfriend for cheating on you. Bank and store robberies were also up there in the rankings, especially if you had to fight security guards or other armed personnel. At the bottom of the list was child molesting, rape, and other crimes where the victim was helpless and there was no provocation.

I got to know Carlos fairly well. At the time, I was nineteen and he was in his upper twenties, although he looked much younger. He had a fair complexion and a young-looking face with eager eyes. At 5 feet 7 inches he was relatively small for a street thug, but he talked tough and wielded a strong urban accent. I suspected that "Carlos" was not his given name because there was not a trace of Hispanic accent, manner, or culture within him. I have no proof, but I bet he chose the name simply to add to his tough street image. Between the math lessons and during casual time reserved for idle conversation, I learned that he played the guitar and loved pop-jazz music. His favorite album of all time, which also happens to be one of my favorites, is Marvin Gaye's classic *What's Going On.* The album, released in 1971, was one of the first concept albums of the genre. Both sides of the LP contained a continuous sequence of songs that called for peace, social justice, love, and reconciliation.

There was no point in formally tutoring prisoners who were on death row, or who were serving life sentences with no chances of parole. They mostly just wanted a chess companion or someone to talk to—for many, their families had long abandoned them in prison. The several lifers that I met all managed some kind of benign hobby. One grew plants. One cared for goldfish. Another was writing his life story. The surreal juxtaposition of a murderer who cares for goldfish in his prison cell moved me. It was indeed possible for a prisoner to sustain a modicum of civility and quality of life even though he had taken someone else's life and even though he had no prospect of rejoining society. I valued this fact and vowed to pay whatever extra taxes society levies to sustain those with life sentences rather than execute them.

We may never understand the mind of a societal misfit. But for a brief time, I sat a little bit closer and was heartened to learn that beneath all the crime and punishment, a small slice of ambition and humanity remains in sight. Sometimes I need to remind myself that for all my scientific understanding of the stars, many people will forever see them as poetic hooks upon which to place their dreams.

## THE LATER YEARS

The decade of the 1990s happened to enjoy several comets of remarkable note, including Comet Shoemaker-Levy 9, which is arguably the most famous comet in history. Its fame derives not from how bright it was or from how many poets were inspired to write about it, but from its brief and spectacular encounter with the planet Jupiter. At over three hundred times the mass of Earth, and at over ten times our diameter, Jupiter's ability to attract comets is unmatched among the planets in the solar system. During the week of celebrations for the twenty-fifth anniversary of the *Apollo 11* Moon landing, Comet Shoemaker Levy 9, having been crumbled into two dozen pieces during a previous close encounter with Jupiter, slammed, one chunk after another, into the Jovian atmosphere. Because Jupiter rotates quickly (once every ten hours), each piece of the comet plunged into a different location of the planet as the atmosphere rotated by. The gaseous scars were easily seen from Earth with ordinary backyard telescopes.

In this game of interplanetary billiards, by far the most dangerous impactor is the long-period comet, which are those with periods greater than two hundred years. Representing about one fourth of Earth's total risk from all possible impactors, long-period comets fall toward the inner solar system from great distances and achieve speeds in excess of a hundred thousand miles per hour by the time they reach Earth. A trip from New York to L.A. at that speed would take all of ninety seconds. Long-period comets thus achieve much higher impact energy for their size than your run-of-the-mill asteroid. More important, they are too dim over most of their orbit to be reliably tracked. By the time we discover a long-period comet headed our way, we might have anywhere from several months to two years to fund, design, build, launch, and intercept it.

For example, in 1996 the Japanese amateur astronomer Yoshii Hyakutake discovered a comet while searching with a tripod-mounted, jumbo pair of binoculars. More than anywhere else on the sky, comet hunters of the world search along a band in the heavens that traces the plane of the solar system. All things considered, the plane is where the action is—planets and asteroids and many comets orbit the Sun close to this plane. But Comet Hyakutake came upon us like a tomahawk from nearly ninety degrees outside of the plane—while nobody was looking. Comets gain considerable speed as they near the Sun, but when viewed from afar, looming in Earth's night sky, this rate instead looks rather stately, just as a distant, fast-moving airplane appears to move slowly overhead.

Bright comets typically enjoy at least a year of hype before they become visible to the naked eye. When Hyakutake was discovered, only three months would pass before the comet would reach its closest approach to Earth—about ten million miles—one of the closest comets on record. This hair's-width distance rendered the comet large and visible in the night sky. The comet could even be seen (with the unaided eye) from the middle of light-polluted Times Square in New York City. After the disappointments of Comet Kohoutek of the 1970s and Comet Halley of the 1980s, we were finally rewarded with a "once-in-a-lifetime" comet.

The Shoemaker-Levy impact with Jupiter was hard to ignore. In July of 1994, I was three years out of my Ph.D. and I had just joined the Hayden Planetarium as a half-time staff scientist, split with Princeton. I was asked at the time to give the keynote address to several hundred supporters of the Astronauts Memorial Foundation (AMF), located at the Kennedy Space Center in Florida. The occasion was a joint celebration of *Apollo 11*'s twenty-fifth anniversary and the dedication of the AMF's newly built Center for Space Education. A year earlier I had been elected as the youngest member to its Board of Directors, which included some executives from Grumman and Lockheed, some influential Floridians, and an astronaut or two from the Apollo and space shuttle eras.

The local industry and culture live symbiotically with the successes and failures of the space program. Many of the region's hotels, scattered throughout Florida's "space coast," feature the twenty-four-hour NASA cable channel on monitors in the lobbies and the hotel rooms. The local newspapers routinely report on NASA politics, NASA funding trends, and on the launch of everything from tiny weather satellites to the space shuttle. I was somewhat apprehensive about my keynote address because the audience's universe was very different from my own. Historically, NASA had very little presence in the American Northeast, my birthplace. There are no major research campuses, no launch sites, no museums of space technology.

Space exploration is generally a good thing, but while my formative years were coincident with NASA's Mercury, Gemini, and Apollo programs, I am far from being a space zealot. I saw who was going into space. The astronauts were predominantly military officers representing the branches of the armed forces. There were no women anywhere in the pipeline, and the chosen ones all wore crew cuts at the same time the musical *Hair!* was enjoying 1,750 performances on Broadway. Furthermore, they all seem to have been selected for their steel nerves and their absence of emotional expression. As far as I could tell, the American agenda was not the exploration of space but the American *conquest* of space to gain military advantage. This was no secret to well-read adults, but to me it was a slow revelation. So the entire enterprise offered little resonance with my own interests and ambitions. After searching for meaningful things to say to this audience of space enthusiasts and educators, I managed to invoke Comet Shoemaker-Levy's impending collision with Jupiter as part of a wake-up call for what could (and perhaps should) sustain a funding trend for the American space program.

In spite of my mild misgivings, I am the first to admit that nothing in this world has the power to inspire forward thinking and visions of the future the way the space program can. The platinum age of space exploration was no doubt the 1960s, but enthusiasm for space was somewhat muddled in many urban centers due to the widespread poverty, urban riots, and poor educational systems. Decades later, the meaning and significance of the space program continues to remain muddled in many urban centers because of a perennial deficit of resources.

But there is a fundamental difference.

In the 1960s, the technology of the future was something that everybody participated in. We were soon all going to be drinking Tang, flitting about in bubble cars and on monorails, and visiting Moon bases on holiday. However flighty yesterday's visions of the future were, today the pastime of imagining the reachable future has been lost.

I still remember the day and the moment when the *Apollo 11* astronauts landed on the Moon. I happened to be with my influential childhood friend from the Skyview apartments where I grew up. We were visiting his relatives in Virginia that summer. The Moon landing was, of course, one of technology's greatest moments. At ten years of age, however, I found myself somewhat indifferent to the event. Not because I couldn't appreciate the moment's rightful place in human history, but because I had every reason to believe that trips to the Moon would become a monthly occurrence. It started with President Kennedy's speech in which he declared that before the decade was over we would send a man to the Moon and return him safely to Earth. Then there was the ongoing space program, with each mission more ambitious than the last. And then, of course, there was Stanley Kubrick's visionary film

*2001: A Space Odyssey,* with its space stations and Moon bases. When you add all this together, it was perfectly clear to me that voyages to the Moon were simply the next step.

Little did I know that they were to become our last steps out of Earth's orbit. In retrospect, I now regret that I did not feel more emotion back on July 20, 1969. I should have reveled in the landing as the singular achievement that it turned out to be.

In spite of the adventure-romance of the Moon landings and sci-fi films, the funding stream for the space program had been primarily defense driven. Cosmic dreams and the innate human desire to explore the frontier are just not as effective at raising $100 billion to go to the Moon as a Cold War enemy and the mandate of a beloved, assassinated President. The continental United States is, at the moment, under relatively little risk of military attack or invasion from a hostile foe. Maybe America needs a new enemy empire to resurrect the catalyst for the limitless flow of funds into the defense and space industries.

Suppose we interpret the word "defense" to mean something far more important than what standing armies and arsenals can bring. Suppose defense means not the defense of political borders but the defense of the human species itself. One needn't look far for a fast lesson in survival. When Comet Shoemaker-Levy 9 slammed into Jupiter's upper atmosphere it unleashed an equivalent energy of 200,000 megatons of TNT on the planet. At ten trillion times the destructive energy of the Hiroshima atomic bomb, this sort of collision, if it happened on Earth, would swiftly render the human species extinct.

If we retain the "defense of the human species" as a mission theme, then we have a genuine cosmic vision to share with today's ten-year-old children. And it's better than bubble cars and monorails. They can be charged with saving life as we know it. We must first acquire a thorough understanding of Earth's climate and ecosystem, which will help to minimize the risk of self-destruction. Second, we must colonize space in as many places as possible, which will proportionally reduce the chance of our annihilation from a collision between Earth and a comet or asteroid; we would then no longer have all our eggs in one basket.

The fossil record teems with extinct species—species of life that had thrived far longer than the current Earth tenure of *Homo sapiens*. Dinosaurs are on this list. The chunks of Comet Shoemaker-Levy 9 were so large, and they were moving so fast, that each hit Jupiter with the equivalent energy of the dinosaur-killing collision between Earth and an asteroid sixty-five million years ago. Whatever damage Jupiter sustained, one thing is for sure: It's got no dinosaurs left.

Dinosaurs are extinct today because they lacked opposable thumbs and the brainpower to build a space program. There would be no greater tragedy in the history of life in the universe than humans becoming extinct—and not because we lack the intelligence to build interplanetary spacecraft. The tragedy would be that the human species itself chose not to fund such a survival plan. The dominant species that replaces us in post-apocalyptic Earth just might wonder why we fared no better than the proverbially pea-brained dinosaurs.

We may still have an opportunity to impart our long-lost visions of the future upon the aspirations of the next generation. If you are one of those who have lost all hope in the "youth of today," then you are not alone in either space or time. Adult complaints about degenerate kids span millennia. Consider the following:

> *The earth is degenerating these days. Bribery and corruption abound. Children no longer mind parents . . . and it is evident that the end of the world is approaching fast.*
>
> ASSYRIAN TABLET ENGRAVED IN 2800 B.C.

If kids were really degenerating from generation to generation then over the thousands of years you would think that civilization should have collapsed long ago.

So it can't be as bad as people think. We just need creative ways to inspire them.

When I was a student in elementary school and junior high school in New York City, I eagerly attended monthly public lectures given by visiting experts on various topics on the universe at the Hayden Planetarium. The speakers were so smart and knew so much that I wanted to be just like them when I grew up. Fifteen years later, I returned to the planetarium to deliver an invited public lecture of the same monthly series that I had attended as a student. Immediately following my lecture, as if I had passed through a loop in the space-time continuum, a twelve-year-old student walked up to me after my lecture and asked, "What should I do to be just like you?" At that moment, I knew that I had helped to plant a dream in someone else the way others before had planted a dream in me. Which reminds me of a few lines from a poem that my parents first read to me when I was seven:

*Hold fast to dreams*
*For if dreams die*
*Life is a broken-winged bird*
*That cannot fly.*

LANGSTON HUGHES

Comet Shoemaker-Levy 9 and its collision with Jupiter was an omen, just as comets were in ancient times. But this omen was in the form of a shot across spaceship Earth's bow. It's the type of news that can shock us into new paradigms, where our investment in the next generation's dreams of space exploration becomes our species' life insurance policy. Equipped with such a policy, we can be fearless in the face of an asteroid with our name on it because only then will we avoid the fate of that broken-winged bird that cannot fly.

A year after the impact of Shoemaker-Levy 9 on Jupiter, another comet of high anticipation came around the Sun. Comet Hale-Bopp had been independently discovered by the professional astronomer Alan Hale and the amateur astronomer Thomas Bopp two years earlier, when it was farther away from Earth than any previous comet had been discovered. We knew Hale-Bopp had to be big for it to be seen so far out in the solar system, but would it be bright? Checking in at over twenty miles in diameter, its nucleus was the largest ever seen. As it neared Earth and the Sun, Hale-Bopp got brighter and brighter until it too became a "once-in-a-lifetime" comet. Hale-Bopp broke all records for remaining brighter than the detection limit of the unaided eye for longer than any other comet on record.

During the several months that Hale-Bopp was at its prettiest, I happened to be taking a cross-country flight in the early evening from New York City to Los Angeles. While cruising at thirty-seven thousand feet above sea level, I looked outside my coach-class window and saw comet Hale-Bopp, bright and beautiful, quietly suspended in the dusk sky. This particular daily flight chases the setting Sun in the west. But even at a speed of six hundred miles per hour, you are guaranteed to lose this race—the "ground speed" rotation of Earth at the latitude of Los Angeles is about nine hundred miles per hour. The plane nonetheless travels fast enough to greatly prolong the majesty of twilight, and anything suspended within it.

The sight of Comet Hale-Bopp sufficiently moved me that I wanted to share my excitement with all two hundred people on board the Boeing 767. Since pilots love to interrupt tranquil flights with miscellaneous announcements, I knew my efforts would be best served if channeled through them. I carefully jotted down a dozen info bits about the comet. Aside from the basic facts of how and when Hale-Bopp was discovered, I took the risk of including one or two apocalyptic facts. For example, the comet is somewhat larger than the asteroid that took out the dinosaurs sixty-five million years ago. If Hale-Bopp were ever to hit Earth, humans would become extinct too. As it penetrated Earth's atmosphere, Hale-Bopp would first create a blast wave that would incinerate over one hundred thousand square miles of vegetation sur-rounding ground zero. Next it would hit Earth's crust, squashing like a bug anything beneath it. Next it would leave a four hundred-mile-diameter crater. The time from first contact with Earth's upper atmosphere until the full excavation of a crater takes about ten seconds. The excavation of the crater would thrust a trillion tons of dust into the stratosphere, plunging Earth into darkness, knocking out the base of the food chain, and rendering over ninety percent of the world's species extinct.

To this page of jotted information I attached my two business cards, one as director of the Hayden Planetarium and the other as research astrophysicist at Princeton University. I pressed the call button, handed the neatly folded lesson plan to the flight attendant, and said, "Please deliver this message to the pilot." I can't explain why, but that was awfully fun to say. It probably ranks with the act of slipping a note to a bank teller.

Sure enough, about five minutes later the pilot made a plane-wide announcement that an astrophysicist on board had supplied him with miscellaneous information about Comet Hale-Bopp that he would like to share with everybody. Part of the crew's job is to ensure the safety of its passengers, which, I think, normally includes their mental safety as well. I was therefore delightfully surprised when the pilot read aloud every line of information from my folded note, including the part about a comet impact's having the capacity to cause the extinction of our species. Apparently everybody was so intrigued by the information that the flight attendant came back down the aisle, invited me to sit up in first class, and served me a mini bottle of champagne followed by an ice-cream sundae. Not since I was fourteen had I been unexpectedly paid and treated to champagne for willingly sharing my knowledge of the universe.

Most of the pedagogical excursions in my life have been with students (junior high through college) and the general public. Only rarely do I get the chance to talk to teachers, although I love nothing more. Apart from generally being an enthusiastic and friendly lot, they shape the conduit of our nation's brain trust. Along the way, they work in the trenches while the rest of us sit at home with a TV remote control in our palm and bark out complaints about the state of the educational system. The nation's teachers are collectively underappreciated, under-respected, and underpaid, but they are not all created equal.

I have always maintained good records of my academic performance throughout my kindergarten through high school years in the public schools of New York City. A small personalized book called *Neil's School Years* facilitated my effort to do so. A gift from my grandmother when I was in third grade, the book invites the owner to record all kinds of academic information, year by year, as you move through school. Pocket folders for each year allow you to save report cards, exams, and small art projects. As I look back on the comment boxes that teachers use when they have more to say than your grade assignment, I notice that evaluations of me are consistent in their complaints about my uncontainable social energy. Most teachers probably assumed that I would one day be pumping gas somewhere, given that I was no one's model student.

The best schoolteachers evaluate the entire talent set represented within each student and they help explore career paths that align with the student's interests. The worst teachers simply issue statements that pass judgment on your behavior in the attempt to homogenize it with the rest of the class.

When I was asked to give a keynote speech in Washington, D.C., to the 1998 winners of the Presidential Award for Excellence in Mathematics and Science Teaching, I gladly accepted the invitation. I owed these star elementary school teachers all I could possibly give.

That evening, I brought with me *Neil's School Years* and noted that for each grade, the book allowed you to check a box identifying what you want to be when you grow up. The six options for boys were Fireman, Policeman, Cowboy, Astronaut, Soldier, Baseball Player. For girls there was Mother, Nurse, School Teacher, Airline Hostess, Model, and Secretary. How a girl could become a mother but a boy could not become a father was a great biological mystery to me at the time, but let's ignore the period sexism.

When I was in kindergarten, during one of the weekly art periods, I drew a nighttime scene using a black crayon to depict the night sky. (For years I never knew what to draw with that pink-colored crayon called "flesh.") Upon seeing my refrigerator art, the teacher politely insisted that the night sky should have been drawn dark blue. I was not swayed and left my teacher with the burden of proof. Two days later she conceded the nighttime black after investigating the problem further. This was the first time I can remember when I was right and the teacher was wrong, which is far more severe than the teacher simply not knowing. I had not expected such an incident to happen until at least junior high school.

On my third-grade report card the teacher wrote, "Neil should cultivate a more serious attitude toward his school work."

My fourth-grade teacher wrote nothing in any of the school

quarters. I don't know which is worse, writing nothing or lodging a complaint in the form of lightly shrouded advice.

My fifth-grade teacher wrote something good followed by something bad. "Neil is a good leader. He shows that he respects the rights, dignity, and feelings of others. He is somewhat lax about completing his work, compositions, notebook, etc. He has to be encouraged and prodded."

That year also happened to be when my geography exam contained a two-part question, beginning "What is the smallest continent?" My correct answer was "Australia." The follow-up question asked, "In what hemisphere is the smallest continent?" I replied "Southern" and it was marked wrong. The "correct" answer was "Eastern." Now there's a teacher who would have never been eligible for the Presidential Award for Excellence.

In all my years of elementary school, nobody ever said, "Neil will go far," or "Neil shows great potential," or "We expect great things from Neil." For that kind of support I needed my parents.

Support is good. But it's best received during times when you think less of yourself than your talents deserve. To be praised for meager or noncompetitive talent just because you are loved does one a disservice in any meritocracy, such as the society in which we live. Whenever that happens, you risk leading a deluded life, where the correspondence between what you deserve for your efforts and what you think you deserve is lost. The value of this "reality check" cannot be overemphasized. Neither Cyril de Grasse Tyson, my father, nor Sunchita Feliciano Tyson, my mother, received formal mathematical, scientific, or technical training in their lives. My father is a sociologist who was active in the civil rights movement of the 1960s, principally as a commissioner under New York City's Mayor John V. Lindsay. And my mother, who returned to school after she raised her children, earned a master's degree in gerontology. Both of them served as a political and social reality check for me, yet they could not directly provide a reality check on my science.

But they did the next best thing. They nurtured my scientific growth.

I must have had the first ever "soccer mom," except the activity wasn't after-school soccer, it was after-school astronomy. With my telescope, camera, and other observing accessories, I would drag both of my parents (separately and together) in and out of cars, up and down stairs, in and out of fields, and to and from the library, all in the support of my astro-habit. I will not soon forget that when I was building my wooden Saturn lamp in seventh grade, my mother and I drove to at least six different hardware stores one afternoon, just to acquire a necessary but unusual electrical fixture.

Furthermore, we were always going to museums, and my parents were always on the lookout for math and science books on the remainder tables of the bookstores. They might have said no. They said no to plenty of other kinds of requests. Had they said no to that which promoted my intellectual growth, my own ability to evaluate what I had previously learned would have been compromised, and I would have lost the capacity to exercise a reality check on myself. It was this capacity that enabled me to know when my talents exceeded the levels they were judged to be by others, and it enabled me not to think too highly of myself in times of gratuitous praise.

My parents never told me where to go or what to learn. In retrospect, that was for the better—because they could not. This ensured that the expressions of my life's interests were as pure as space itself. To this day, my parents remain two of the most warm and caring parents I have known. Of all the places I have been, the troubles I have seen, and the trials I have endured, let there be no doubt that I continually felt their guidance ahead of me, their support behind me, their love beside me.

TWO

# SCIENTIFIC ADVENTURES

### THE FUN AND FRUSTRATIONS OF BEING A SCIENTIST

I'VE WORKED HARD TO EXPOSE MY TODDLER TO THE LAWS OF PHYSICS. Actually, she performs most of the experiments herself. She once dropped twenty-three overcooked peas, one by one, from her dinner plate to the ground. This particular experiment highlighted two principles: the conversion of gravitational potential energy to kinetic energy (the peas gain speed as they fall), and the nature of inelastic collisions (the peas flatten, instead of bounce, as they hit the floor). During her experiments in fluid dynamics, she poured a cup of apple juice into her dinner plate, and then poured it back into her cup. She repeated these actions until all the juice had spilled onto the dinner table. She then watched the puddle drizzle down through the seam in the table's leaves to become a puddle on the floor. After dinner, she climbed down from her booster seat and stepped flat-footed into the puddle, scattering the juice all over. I love it! And yes, I am the one who cleans up after her.

So much of what shapes and comprises what we call "common sense" derives from a careful assessment of the way the world works. So horror descends upon my scientific soul every time my daughter requests to see the Walt Disney classic *Mary Poppins*. The first time I inserted the video into our VCR (remarkably, I had never before seen the film) I did not know what to expect. What unfolded before my eyes thoroughly and purposefully violated nearly all known laws of physics. In Mary Poppins's first appearance in the film, she floats into town holding her outstretched umbrella. Okay, maybe that could happen. But upon entering the children's house (after she gets the offer to be the live-in nanny) Mary Poppins slides *up* the banister and then proceeds to remove from her ten-inch handbag all manner of oversize household trimmings and furniture to make her room and term of employment a bit more comfortable. Later, Mary has a conversation along a London sidewalk with a dog, in which she speaks English and the dog speaks dog. Shortly thereafter, while at Uncle Albert's house, Mary serves tea to all assembled while they are laughing and afloat near the ceiling. When frolicking upon London rooftops, after having been sucked up a chimney, Mary Poppins creates stairs through the air out of ascending chimney smoke that spans from one building to the next. She then leads a procession across it. And at the end of the film Mary has a conversation with the bird head that forms the end of her umbrella handle.

Not long ago, Mary Poppins would surely have been burned at the stake for being a witch. Now she is a cherished Disney icon. My daughter must now reconcile her own nascent common sense with a story that mocks the laws of physics. Perhaps I shouldn't single out *Mary Poppins*. *Alice's Adventures in Wonderland* is no better—except that Wonderland offers no pretense of being in downtown London. The same goes for Never Never Land in *Peter Pan*, which is off behind a star somewhere* and Munchkin Land in the *Wizard of Oz*, which, we are reminded, is not in Kansas.

At the risk of sounding like a curmudgeon, allow me to say that one of society's greatest ills is the astonishing breadth and depth of its scientific (and mathematical) illiteracy. Just listen to the circuitous reasoning that some people invoke to justify why one should not wear seat belts while driving: They are too restrictive; they are too uncomfortable; seat belts are for sissies. When the explanations are over, ask the drivers whether they have ever taken a high school or college-level physics class. The answer will be no. College physics is where you learn about inertia and see demonstrations of Isaac Newton's famous law, "Things in motion tend to stay in motion unless acted upon by an outside force." If you do not wear a seat belt, a head-on collision will smash your face into the windshield at the same speed the car was traveling. In a curious revenge of physical laws, while not all taxis will stop to pick me up on the street corner in favor of a White person farther down the block many of these same drivers don't buckle their seat belts either.

No, I do not blame all science illiteracy on Disney, or on Hollywood, as is customary for other problems of society. But I do blame it on how cavalierly society treats skills that promote critical thinking—the kind of thinking that enables you to

---

*The exact directions are "Second star to the right, straight on until morning."

use the scientific laws of nature to judge whether someone else is a crackpot. Children in kindergarten and elementary school routinely take art classes that promote creativity instead of taking classes that explore how Nature works. Just look at the horizontal and vertical display surfaces in the homes of parents with young children—refrigerator doors included. The pasta collages will far outnumber the science experiments. Children are also encouraged to read fantasies and fairy tales in which, as best as I can tell, there are no laws of Nature at work. Yet we all sit back and wonder how cults can form, how billions of dollars per year can be spent on astrologers and psychics, and how innocent people can be bilked of their savings by paranormal swindlers.

In a recent story in the *New York Times** the headline reads "A Police Sting Cracks Down on Fortune-telling Fraud." The article recounts several cases of people who were convinced by a fortune-teller that they were cursed or otherwise diseased, requiring for a cure multiple visits, questionable herbal treatments, and large sums of money. One woman in particular had trouble sleeping, and to her credit, first went to physicians, psychiatrists, and priests. But when none of them could offer help, she visited a fortune-teller, who diagnosed her as having "a lot of negativity in her aura." The fortune-teller prescribed a root remedy that required a trip to the Middle East to obtain. Of course it was the fortune-teller who made the trip—at the woman's expense. Three thousand dollars later, the woman suspected fraud and went to the police. What strikes me hardest about this story is that the woman, who owns an insurance

*New York Times*, Wednesday, June 16, 1999. Metro Section, Page B1.

agency, is quoted as saying, "I am not naïve or unintelligent. . . ."

I don't know how many critical thinking skills are required to be a good insurance agent. You might hope there are a few. They insure you, your loved ones, and your property, so perhaps some math and logic would be involved in this effort. She exhibited no critical thinking skills, yet assumed she had.

Here are a few things the woman did *not* say:

> *"Gee, if I had been more skeptical of the fortune-
> teller then I wouldn't have gotten robbed."*
> *"I had a temporary lapse of judgment that won't
> happen again."*
> *"Society has duped me into thinking I am intelli-
> gent even though I have hardly any capacity
> to evaluate the statements and claims of others."*

Suppose the woman were a lawyer instead of an insurance executive? Suppose it was her turn to be a juror? What would then happen within the legal system? I cannot speak for the federal courts, but I gleaned some insight to these questions during my first stint on jury duty in Manhattan's County Court. Having never, until recently, spent more than several years in the same place, or even the same municipality, during my adult life, I had never been called for jury duty, which typically requires a minimum duration of residency. All I knew of courtroom drama was what I watched on prime-time television, featuring eloquent lawyers and swayable jurors. When I was finally called to serve, in November of 1997, I had been a resident of Manhattan for three years. I went willingly and patriotically. I even got dressed up in my best academic tweed. In anticipation of a long wait in the waiting room I brought my laptop computer and newspapers to read.

About fifty of us were there, some of whom looked impatient and haggard. They were in their third and final day of waiting. Others, like me, were freshly pressed and wide-eyed. The waiting room happened to have a running television perched in the corner, but it was mounted so high that nobody could reach it to change the channel. And no telling where the remote was. I don't watch much daytime television, so I cannot distinguish the normal from the unusual. But on that day, and at that time, there was a Jerry Springer marathon of four consecutive hours. I had never before seen Jerry Springer's talk show and I knew nothing about his interview philosophies or his choice of guests.

We were all there, pretending to do important work at the tables and on the couches of the waiting room. And we were all trying to ignore the television when all of a sudden two of the talk show guests broke into a fistfight. Our eyes were transfixed and our mouths were agape. I assumed the fight to be a rare moment. Nope. The next set of guests also broke into a fight. I forgot why. Maybe it was the one where somebody's transvestite boyfriend had a secret love affair with the girlfriend's father. We all sat there and watched guest after guest, fight after fight, episode after episode. And we shamelessly cheered the emotional outbursts of each guest who, by our judgment, had been wronged. By early afternoon, I was finally called for the juror selection process, but not without having borne witness to the most lawless show on television in the hallowed halls of New York City's criminal courthouse.

After a shorter wait outside an actual courtroom, the presiding judge invited a group of us inside for attorney questioning. As others went before me, I was fascinated by the questions and the answers—all attempting to probe whatever biases we might have toward the defendant, who was present and in full view with his lawyer. What might they ask me? What biases might I have? One thing is for sure; they were hell-bent on probing everyone's livelihood. At the time, I happened to be co-teaching (via guest lectures) a possibly relevant seminar at Princeton University. The questioning attorney began:

> *What is your profession?*
> Astrophysicist.
> *What is an astrophysicist?*
> An astrophysicist studies the universe and the laws
> of physics that describe and predict its behavior.
> *What sorts of things do you do?*
> Research, teach, administrate.
> *What courses do you teach?*
> This semester I happen to be teaching a seminar at
> Princeton University on the critical evaluation of
> scientific evidence and the relative unreliability of
> human testimony.
> *No further questions your honor.*

I was on my way home twenty minutes later.

I suppose I should have been happy to be dismissed. It meant I could go back to work, or go back home and spend time with my family. But I was upset. Not for myself but for our legal system that eschews rational thought. It became easy for me to understand how O. J. Simpson, and the police who beat Rodney King, could both be acquitted in the face of strong evidence against them. Emotional truths woven by lawyers in the court of law are apparently more important than the truths of actual events. I have grown to fear for those whose innocence has become trapped within the legal system.

From what I know of courts of law, during the questioning of witnesses, yes/no and multiple choice questions are common. But the laws of physics do not lend themselves to such responses without incurring a major misrepresentation of reality. In my first year as a staff scientist at the Hayden Planetarium, I was called by a lawyer who wanted to know what time the Sun set on the date of a particular car accident at a particular location. This question can be answered precisely, but later in the conversation I learned what that lawyer really wanted to know was what time it got dark outside. He was going to compare the time of sunset with the time of the car accident, and had been assuming that everything gets dark the instant the Sun dips below the horizon. His question was poorly formed for the information he was seeking. A better question might have been, what time do the dark-sensitive street lights turn on? But even for that question, the presence or absence of clouds and the shadows of nearby buildings can affect the "right" answer.

Although I was tainted goods in the jury selection box, on another occasion I managed to help convict a person who was charged with a fatal hit-and-run. The driver of the vehicle had a photograph of himself, claiming it was taken at the time of the incident and that he was nowhere near the scene of the crime. The defense attorney asked me if I could verify the claimed time of the image from the lengths of shadows laid by cars and people in the photo. I said sure. If the exact date and location of the crime are known, then there exists only one time of day for which the Sun will create a shadow of a given length in a given direction of a given object. Armed with some handy software on the Sun, Moon, and planets, I made simple measurements of the shadows within the photograph and I provided the lawyer with the time of the photo, plus or minus twelve minutes. The suspect's alibi was off by several hours. I suppose he never knew what I had known since age fourteen: that in the courthouse of the universe, the laws of physics do not lie, nor are they influenced by anybody's emotional state, and they apply equally to everyone.

When scientists invoke the scientific method, our ways are not as mysterious or as foreign as you might presume. The scientific method forces the researcher to go to any extreme necessary to minimize bias during the acquisition and interpretation of data. The biggest source of error and bias in the acquisition of data happens to be the person who conducts the experiment. A researcher's mood, attitude, political leanings, bigotry, and prejudice have all influenced the integrity of scientific data in the past. The most famous deluded experimenter in the history of astronomy was Percival Lowell. In his studies of the planet Mars he "saw" networks of canals connecting areas of polar water supplies to vegetation and cities. The entire public works project was presumed to be built by intelligent Martians. Lowell drew detailed maps of what he saw and instigated an entire generation of fantasies about life in the universe. This episode would be laughable were it not for Lowell's otherwise distinguished reputation as a first-rate astronomer, best known for launching the systematic search for planet X, which led to the discovery of Pluto. Without chart recorders, photographs, or other means to document Mars's appearance, the severe shortcomings of Lowell's very human senses were readily revealed.

Why, then, in the court of law is eyewitness testimony among the most coveted forms of evidence? One or more eye-witnesses can send you to your death. At least nobody ever died from biased data in astrophysics.

Sometimes ignorance of the laws of physics can have inno-cent and even playful consequences. From eleventh grade through the middle of graduate school I invested my principal athletic energies in the sport of wrestling. Not to the exclusion of training my mind, but I was nonetheless serious about my athletic commitment for reasons (I would later learn) that had less to do with my personal athletic ambitions than societal ex-pectations. I was captain of my high school's team and wres-tled varsity in college at the 190-pound weight class, where there was good incentive to not gain a single pound because the next higher category was "Unlimited."

Many sports represent extreme physical challenges such as rowing, swimming, and cross-country skiing. But if you have ever wrestled, you will say that wrestling was the most taxing sport you have ever attempted. All you need to do is turn your opponent so that his back lies against the wrestling mat for about one second. Then you win. An entire match lasts eight minutes. To be good at it, all your muscles must be strong, especially those of the upper body. You must also be flexible, quick, and have near-infinite physical stamina. Lastly, you must intuitively understand vector diagrams from the laws of physics. Knowing balance points, tipping points, strength points, weak points, center of mass, and leverage points are all factors in moving your opponent to his back. I qualified on most counts, although I was almost too flexible. I was quicker than practically all my opponents. And I certainly knew my force diagrams. My average opponent, however, was four inches shorter. Since we weighed the same (190 pounds), under what was essentially no body fat, my opponent's muscles were therefore always larger. I was consistently the weaker wrestler, since biophysics dictates that muscle strength is proportional to muscle cross section. My task was to stay clear of vise-grip muscle holds and to keep my center of mass from getting too high relative to my opponent. My opponent's task was to tame and outmaneuver my long and unwieldy limbs.

In the early 1990s, after completing my Ph.D. from Columbia University, I was appointed as a postdoctoral research associate at Princeton University's Department of Astrophysical Sciences, which was all somewhat later than my wrestling prime. I would nonetheless occasionally roll around with the varsity team. In the third year of my three-year postdoctoral appointment, PBS filmed me for a multipart series titled *Breakthrough: The Changing Face of Science in America,* which profiled a dozen or so active scientists from underrepresented ethnic backgrounds. I was featured for seventeen minutes in the one-hour episode titled "Path of the Most Resistance," the title of which was selected by the producers from a line in my 1991 Ph.D. Convocation Speech at Columbia University. My episode profiled two physicists and two astrophysicists. Part of the program's intent was to give the viewer a full picture of the life and times of the featured scientists. Which means in my case showing some gratuitously embarrassing baby pictures and home movies from my childhood. The producers and film crew also trailed me to the Andes Mountains of South America, where they documented my multi-night observing session on telescopes at the Cerro Tololo Inter-American Observatory.

Back on campus, they also wanted footage of me working out with the Princeton University wrestling team. Unfortunately, the cinematographer had never filmed wrestlers before, and apparently didn't know much physics either. He could not reliably determine when a wrestling hold would lead to one or the other wrestler's advantage. During the sparring sessions there was one move that I had started on top, but I planted my center of mass too high and my support points became controlled by my opponent. I executed a failed hold on my opponent's arms and torso that ending in my getting flipped to my back and pinned. Sure enough, this was the segment they edited into the program, and it was viewed by millions of people. When I asked the producer about it later he replied, "But you looked like you had him!"

Being a good or even average wrestler ensured that I was in good physical condition for more than fifteen years of my adult life. This fact apparently did not go unnoticed by the Public

Information Office of Columbia University, which tracked me down in Princeton to recruit me for the 1997 "Studmuffins of Science" Calendar. The invitation arrived via e-mail.

Date: Mon, 19 Feb 1996 11:33:07 -0500 (EST)
From: Robert J Nelson <rjn2@columbia.edu>
To: ndt@astro.Princeton.EDU

Subject: Studly Scientists

Hi Neil!
Bob Nelson here at Columbia University's Office of Public Information.

You may have heard of the Science Studmuffins calendar. Karen Hopkin, a producer for Science Friday on NPR, did this calendar for 1996 and is back looking for more scientists to appear next year. Let me immediately add that everyone wears clothes in this particular calendar and I have one hanging in my office at Columbia. Although Ms. Hopkin emphasizes physical attractiveness, I think she's looking for well-rounded scientists (well, probably not in the physical sense!!) who have diverse interests and give the lie to nerd stereotypes.

Anyway, if you're interested, let me know, or maybe the PR office at Princeton will be interested.

Cordially,
Bob Nelson
Office of Public Information and Communications
Columbia University

My e-mail reply was brief:

From: Neil deGrasse Tyson <ndt@astro. Princeton.EDU>

Date: Fri, 8 Mar 1996 18: 52: 53 0500

To: rjn2@columbia.edu

Subject: Studly Scientists

Dear Bob,

Thank you for the flattering invitation to participate in the 1997 "Studmuffins of Science" calendar.

I have worked hard to be respected for my mind rather than my body. I believe I have finally succeeded, and thus do not wish to jeopardize my long-fought efforts.

Good luck, nonetheless, in your recruitment.

Sincerely

Neil deGrasse Tyson

Princeton Astrophysics

I remain flattered by the request but have no regrets for declining the invitation. If I wasn't going to dance half nude to "Great Balls of Fire" back in Texas, then I was not going to pose as a studly scientist for a nationally distributed calendar.

Knowledge and execution of the laws of physics can make you appear far more powerful than you actually are. While I was still in graduate school, during the days that followed an astrophysics conference on Italy's Amalfi coast, my wife and I took a local bus on tour of the many shops and restaurants of the nearby towns. As you might expect, the single road that connected all towns was narrow, with many switchback turns that barely negotiated the rocky coast. During one excursion our bus could not enter a town because a car had been sloppily parked, headfirst and askew, on the curb of our tight turn. Our bus honked its horn long and loud, but whoever owned the car was nowhere to be found. Traffic was building. Soon about twenty impatient cars collected behind us, wrapped beyond the previous turn. After ten minutes of futile steering gesticulations by townspeople to our bus driver, he finally gave up. He turned off the bus, sat in the opened doorway, and lit a cigarette. All the while I had been plotting a solution to this dilemma and I had just received my cue. In this part of Italy, few people were within four inches of my height, fifty pounds of my weight, or within one hundred shades of my skin color. So I stood out just by being there. But now I would be remembered forever. I stood up and walked to the front of the bus. Exited. Walked over to the problem car. Bent down and dead-lifted its rear section with a firm double grip on its bumper. I then slid the car sideways about three feet, providing adequate clearance for the bus to proceed. The forty or so people who were on the scene had stared silently at me during the episode. After I had moved the car they spontaneously burst into cheers and applause.

I thought nothing of the feat at the time, but reflecting upon it later I surmised that it might be the stuff of local legends. It had all the ingredients of a story that would pass from generation to generation. And it would not be immune to exaggeration. I can see it now. "The Legend of the Strong Man: A stranger from Ethiopia came to our town who was as large as an ox. He was the silent type. No one knew his name. He was a drifter. But just when he had arrived, the parking brakes of a local bus gave way on the hill. As the bus began to roll, little Giuseppe was crossing the street while holding hands with his grandmother. The Ethiopian stranger reacted quickly by thrusting his massive body in front of the bus, stopping it with his bare hands before he lifted its front end and swung it from its deadly path."

In the first place, European-made cars in small-town coastal Italy hardly weigh anything. Secondly, sloppily parked cars along narrow streets of Europe tend to be parked headfirst, and most of them have engines in the front, so the light end (the rear) is what sticks out to block traffic. A human can raise more weight with a dead lift than with practically any other unassisted method. In dead lift, you invoke primarily the muscles in your thigh, the body's strongest, and neither your shoulders, your arms, nor your back actually do work against the force of gravity. The world record dead lift is about half a ton. Using a dead lift to raise the light end of a car is not as easy as raising the light end of a wheel barrow, but it comes close.

The friction between rubber and concrete is among the highest between any two surfaces, which means if you want to slide a car sideways on a road then you must apply nearly as much sideways force as the weight of the car itself. An essentially impossible task. The secret is to apply an upward force on the rear of the car until the weight on its tires is less than your own weight. You can then nudge the car, inch by inch, in whatever direction your traffic needs require. The car probably weighed fifteen hundred pounds (tops) with two thirds of that weight sitting primarily over its front tires. By applying an upward force of two or three hundred pounds, sliding the car sideways became a trivial exercise in the laws of physics.

I have not gone back to see if the local townspeople erected any statues to commemorate the perceived feat of strength. But enough time has elapsed (more than a decade) for the story to have become legend, if it's destined to become a legend at all.

With the major network news headquarters located less than a mile from the Hayden Planetarium, I am an easy date for them to get a quick sound-byte on the latest discoveries in the universe. In February of 1996, the discovery of a new extra-solar planet was announced, and ABC News sent a crew up to the Hayden to solicit my comments for the evening news with anchor Peter Jennings. My comments would be part of a larger story on the subject that included interviews with the discoverers themselves and others. We do not observe extra-solar planets directly. We infer their presence from gravitational effects on the host star, which we observe as a wobble in the star's position in space. I offered the interviewer one of my best explanations for how you deduce the existence of a planet from the Doppler shift of the star's spectrum. I further commented that the star's wobble in reaction to the planet's gravity is more accurately described as a jiggle, and I reenacted what the star does using my hips.

In spite of what I thought was an erudite explanation of the discovery, perhaps expecting one or two sound-bytes to be extracted, all the news showed of me that evening was my jiggling hips. For media interviews, I have since refrained from using my body to assist my explanations of scientific phenomena.

Just a few month's later, in May of 1996, NASA presented the discovery of evidence for life on Mars, embedded in a Martian meteorite found on Earth. The day *before* the life-on-the-Mars-rock story was formally announced by NASA, I was coincidentally in Washington, D.C. with other high-level administrators from the American Museum of Natural History to plumb for mutually beneficial projects with NASA in a meeting at their headquarters. There are many museums across the land, and NASA had no particular reason to presume that we were different or special. Our encounter with NASA officials was polite and cordial.

On our way out of the NASA headquarters, the cell phone of one of our team members rang. It was the Communications Department of the Museum. They received an inquiry from ABC's *Nightline* about a major discovery on Mars, and enquired whether I would be interested in appearing that night to discuss it. I knew the positions of all NASA's space probes in the solar system at that moment, and none of them were positioned to make any breakthrough discovery about Mars. After fifteen minutes of phone calls between us and the museum and between the museum and the *Nightline* producers, I was able to glean that NASA was going to announce that extraterrestrial life may have been discovered on Mars. For this to happen I knew immediately it could only have come from the analysis of meteorites. I agreed to do the interview provided that I could be supplied with the original research paper and time enough to study the results. The major networks—in almost every case where I am called upon to comment on a cosmic discovery—will have also interviewed the scientists responsible for the results. This frees me to offer big-picture perspectives on the role and meaning of the discoveries to the typical viewer.

No time remained to fly back to New York City that evening and be interviewed, so I was interviewed at the ABC affiliate studios in Washington, representing the Hayden Planetarium of the American Museum of Natural History. The segment producer handed to me what looked like a bootlegged galley of the original research paper and I had about ninety minutes to study it. You should know that the paper was professionally researched, and was written with language that was as humble and tentative about the findings as you could imagine, but you would never know it from the headlines that were to come.

The next day the President of the United States, in a move I had never before seen, introduced the NASA press conference from the lawn of the White House. The head of NASA gave an introduction of his own that included one or two scientific recollections from his childhood, including trips with his father to New York City's Hayden Planetarium. I don't know if he would have mentioned the Hayden anyway or if he mentioned it only because we were in his face the day before, but it was a warm gesture felt by all New Yorkers who were watching.

The day of the NASA press conference, the *CBS Evening News* interviewed the head of NASA, the lead author of the research paper, Carl Sagan by telephone, and me. I was flattered and honored to join that threesome, but I was especially happy to offer comments and perspectives that might further enhance the scientific appreciation for the discovery in the hearts and minds of the millions of Americans who were watching. The media frenzy was, I believe, appropriate to the significance of the news story, although conspiracy skeptics were certain all the hoopla was an overnight stunt to reinvigorate NASA's diminished funding from Congress. NASA funding did receive a small uptick, but the naysayers clearly had not seen the original research paper, which had been years in the making.

I was not alone in my expertise. A half-dozen scientists at the museum had knowledge that could be tapped for interviews about the Mars rock. We have biochemists, meteorite specialists, and solar system experts. And almost weekly, one scientist or another from the dozen research departments is consulted by the media about a breaking scientific story. The American Museum of Natural History is not just another museum.

On another media occasion when the networks were hungry for astrophysicists, the infamous asteroid 1997 XF11 was reported as having a real chance of striking Earth. Predictably, a media frenzy followed. The date was March 11, 1998. Within twenty-four hours, on March 12, the threat of impact was retracted after more detailed calculations became available: The asteroid would miss Earth by six hundred thousand miles. I was promptly called upon by the producers for ABC's *World News Tonight* to explain what the hell had just happened. They wanted their news anchor Peter Jennings to conduct a live, on-air interview, which for me was without precedent.

So I donned my best dark suit, my best French-cuffed shirt, and my favorite astro-novelty tie and showed up at the ABC network studios on West Sixty-seventh Street in Manhattan. Of the fifty or so ties that I own, about two thirds have patterns that evoke astronomical themes. Some are nerdy like the one with a space shuttle being launched straight up the tie. Others are artsy, like the mockup of Vincent van Gogh's *The Starry Night*, complete with the pointy and wavy bush, the church steeple from the town, a few of the fuzzy stars, and the crescent moon—all deftly rearranged to look as though van Gogh had painted them on a two-and-a-half-inch vertical strip of cloth. I own yet another category of astro-tie that is simply loud. This was the category of tie I wore for the Peter Jennings interview. That particular tie displays randomly oriented golden-yellow stars, moons, and comets floating on a satin black background.

During the two-and-a-half-minute interview, Jennings asked about how the asteroid was discovered, why is was initially perceived to be a threat, and why all was now okay. At the end of the interview, Jennings somehow felt compelled to comment. He uttered two simple words in front of his two million viewers: "Nice tie!"

Afterward, on my way out of the studios, no fewer than a dozen people from the production staff, including writers, editors, and camera operators, came up to me to get a closer look at my tie. They were all astonished that Jennings broke script, which they asserted he never does. Over the twenty-four hours that followed, I received dozens of e-mails from all kinds of people—strangers and friends—each offering congratulations on the interview and humorously ending with the identical compliment, "Nice tie!" One e-mail happened to come from my eleventh-grade English teacher, Mr. Bernard Kurtin, who was famous for his witty cynicism. Once, when I cut class on one of the numerous Jewish holidays in September, one of my classmates told me that when he took attendance and noticed my absence, he asked the class, "Where is Rabbi Tyson?" I hadn't seen or heard of Mr. Kurtin since high school. Of the sixty e-mails I receive per day, I will never forget his one-line message the evening of my appearance with Peter Jennings:

Date: Fri, 13 Mar 1998 09:32:36 +0000

To: tyson@astro.amnh.org

From: "Bernard Kurtin" bernzel@email.msn.com>

I thought your necktie was just so, so.

-Bernard Kurtin

I own an asteroid. Rather, I own a piece of an iron-nickel asteroid that slammed into Earth at a speed of several miles per second, was collected by a meteorite hunter, and made its way to an auction house in New York City, where I put forth the winning bid. This particular asteroid fragment weighs a couple of pounds and spans the palm of my hand. Striations across its face betray an explosive episode somewhere in the asteroid's journey through 4.6 billion years. At a gavel price of $1,300 it qualifies as the most expensive paperweight I have ever owned.

At the same auction, there was a second, larger meteorite that piqued my interest. It too was composed of iron-nickel but weighed about fifteen pounds and was the size and proportions of a track and field discus. This particular meteorite had an esthetic quality to its shape—a natural hole had smoothly worn through the center so that when mounted upright, the meteor looked like a stylized doughnut that could easily pass for an objet d'art. Apparently I wanted it more than anybody else in the room, because I soon became the lone bidder against a person who was posting live bids to the auctioneer via telephone from California. The unidentified caller and I leapfrogged right up to my spending limit, and then some, but my pocketbook was evidently no match for the phone bidder's interest level and resources. Several weeks later I learned that my opposing bidder was Steven Spielberg. Clearly, no matter how much money I had planned to spend that afternoon, I was not going home with that meteorite. My disappointment eased, however, when I realized that our generation's greatest film storyteller, the one who brought us *E.T. The Extra-Terrestrial*, shared my interest in acquiring an extraterrestrial of verifiable provenance.

Of the ten thousand or so catalogued asteroids in the solar system, several are visible and trackable with a small telescope. The word "asteroid" translates to "starlike" because, apart from asteroids' incessant motion against the background stars, they look much like ordinary stars through most telescopes. Planets, on the other hand, are bright and clearly identifiable through a telescope as celestial orbs—entire worlds beyond our own.

For most of the year the planets Venus, Mars, Jupiter, and Saturn are brighter than nearly every star in the sky. This means that they tend to be the first to "come out" after sunset. You now have a plausible reason why your wishes generally don't come true whenever you wish upon a star in the early evening sky. The planets visible to the unaided eye orbit the Sun in periods that range from 88 days for Mercury, through 29.5 years for Saturn. From month to month and from year to year, different planets will masquerade as the first star of the evening. Since all the planets orbit close to the plane of the solar system, every now and then two or more of them come into alignment on the sky when viewed from Earth. By alignment I mean within a few degrees each other so that they fit nicely in the field of household binoculars. The alignment of planets is no more rare than the exact configuration of all planets at any arbitrarily selected moment. Planetary alignments just happen to be more beautiful. While I was a postdoctoral research scientist at Princeton University's Department of Astrophysics, I received a phone call from a graduate student in the Chinese Studies department. He was translating an ancient manuscript which chronicled a cosmic event that led to the overthrow of a dynasty. The student suspected that the cosmic event was an alignment of the planets but he wanted verification. So I invited him by.

I own several planetarium-style sky programs that run on my office computers. They all show you the configuration of the Sun, Moon, and planets, for anyplace on Earth and for any time of day, day of the year, and year on the calendar for thousands of years into the past and future. Some programs are better than others and retain their accuracy over a longer base of time. The graduate student translated the Chinese calendar dates and declared that the auspicious cosmic event must have fallen somewhere between 1960 and 1950 B.C. on the Gregorian calendar. To be safe, I conducted a search of planetary alignments over a broader range of years, from 2000 to 1900 B.C. Not knowing which planets would participate, nor what separation would be ominous to the ancient Chinese, I selected for any combination of Jupiter, Venus, and Mars and looked for a mutual separation of less than twenty degrees on the sky. I dropped my calculator when I discovered that during the early morning hours of February 25, 1952 B.C., the five planets visible to the unaided eye—Mercury, Venus, Mars, Jupiter, and Saturn—all fell within a three-degree circle of each other in the dawn sky. If you isolate the planets Mars, Mercury, and Venus, they fit within an even tighter half-degree circle. The three-degree separation is so small that if you held your hand at arm's length, your thumbnail would eclipse all five of them. If people needed an excuse to overthrow a dynasty, they had found it. In my continued searches, no other time from 3000 B.C. to A.D. 3000 produced such an impressive conjunction of the naked-eye planets.

I was fresh off the discovery of the Chinese planetary alignment when the time came to replace the Hayden Planetarium's Zeiss model VI star projector. It had been installed in the late 1960s and was ready for an upgrade. A team of us combed the world for a modern projector to replace it. One such trip was back to Zeiss in their Jena, Germany, headquarters to see a prototype of their latest model VIII projector in their planetarium test dome. In the technological counterpart to kicking a car's tires before you buy it, I asked the engineers to take me to 1952 B.C. This happened to fall outside their test algorithms, but they attempted it anyway. With the naked-eye planet projectors on full zoom and their whirling motion against the background stars in a countdown of years, all planets found each other and huddled together tightly on the morning of February 25. Their engineers were pleased, as was I. I now invoke the Chinese alignment as a test of all software and star projectors that I come to evaluate.

I'm a fan of the planets in any combination. When I was

born, Mercury, Venus, Jupiter, Saturn, Uranus, Neptune, Pluto, the Sun, and Moon were all in the sky. The planets normally bring me good luck—even though I don't believe in luck. But the week before the presidential elections of 1996, the *NBC Nightly News* with Tom Brokaw ran a series of spots called "Fixing America" during which various well-known and unknown people were interviewed for their perspectives on what was wrong with America. The people were further prompted for ideas about how they might remedy the problems. When I was chosen for one of those spots, the camera crew elected to film me in the Sky Theater of the Hayden Planetarium. For the scene, the Zeiss star projector was to my left, and a large, zoomed video image of Saturn was projected on the dome and floating above my right shoulder. I was finally photographed together with my favorite planet. I gave my best advice for the nation that day, declaring that science literacy was good and even necessary for the electorate to make informed decisions about issues in modern society that affect our lives. I went on to declare that public interest in cosmic discovery is high and should serve as a magnet for children's interest in science. When accompanied by Saturn, the subject of my desk lamp, how could anything go wrong with the interview?

These daily "Fixing America" segments typically featured two or three people. Out of curiosity, I asked the producer of the segment who else they were interviewing. I was scheduled to be grouped with a football coach from a midwestern college, and the Metropolitan Opera singer Jessye Norman.

The following day, the segment aired on the news in the sequence Jessye Norman, me, the football coach. The footage of me in the Sky Theater, flanked by Saturn and the star projector, looked otherworldly—as though I were visiting Saturn in its orbit rather than that its image visiting me on Earth. But none of that mattered. Everything that I said was totally eclipsed by Jessye Norman. Her message that day was in direct response to the rhetoric of the Republican presidential hopefuls, who, during that election season, kept referring to how the poor needed to pick themselves up by their bootstraps. Bootstraps became metaphor for programs that would reduce the welfare rolls.

Jessye Norman's visage radiates bright cheeks, a high forehead, and expressive, high-arched eyebrows. Her elocution reminds you of a classical orator. Her dignity, stately manner, and her gown could grace any throne in the world. Her intelligence and clarity of thought were manifest.

Ms. Norman enunciated all her syllables with poetic drama that only an opera singer can deliver: "We should dare to care about one another. We should not allow politicians to suggest that the poor are not our concern. These are the people who are not able to pull themselves up by bootstraps—they are not wearing any boots."

Cut. Print. End segment. End newscast.

The moment she spoke, I knew that my pleas for science literacy would pale by comparison. They should have left me and my Saturn for another day, or another occasion, or on the editing room floor.

Another planet that has figured prominently in my life, especially lately, is Pluto. I published an essay for *Natural History* magazine in February 1999 titled "Pluto's Honor." The time was not arbitrary. That month, Pluto regained its status as the most far out planet after a twenty-year stint orbiting closer to the Sun than Neptune. Pluto's uniquely elongated orbit happens to crosses Neptune's orbit for 20 years out of a 248-year period. In my essay I presented the case for demoting Pluto from its long-held status as a planet to a classification that aligns it more closely with comets found in the outer solar system. The argument is simple. Pluto never really fit into the family of planets. It is the smallest among them—indeed seven moons of other planets (including Earth's Moon) are bigger. More than half Pluto's volume is ice, so that if you brought Pluto closer to the Sun, say, the Earth-Sun distance, then Pluto would grow a hundred-million-mile-long cometary tail. Now what kind of behavior is that for a planet? But the nails in the coffin come from the 1992 discovery of icy bodies beyond the orbit of Neptune that have more properties in common with Pluto (orbit, composition, size, etc.) than either Pluto or these icy bodies have in common with any other planet. We are left with little choice but to give Pluto its walking papers and require that it join this other class of objects. But all is not lost. Pluto would go from being the tiniest planet to being the largest known icy object in the outer solar system.

By about February 10, the mail started rolling in. I knew Pluto was popular among elementary school kids but I had no idea they would mobilize into a "Save Pluto" campaign. I now have a drawerful of hate letters from hundreds of elementary school children (with supportive cover letters from their science teachers) pleading with me to reverse my stance on Pluto. The file includes a photograph of the entire third grade of a school posing on their front steps and holding up a banner proclaiming "Dr. Tyson, Pluto is a Planet!" One of the letters was from the Pluto Protection Society, based near the Lowell

Observatory, Arizona, the home of the original photographic search that led to Pluto's discovery in 1930. And a newspaper article and profile on me, published the following month in the *New York Observer*, led with a small front-page head shot (indicating a larger article within), and the tag line "The Man Who Would Demote Pluto."

The world's arbiter of astronomical nomenclature and classification systems is the International Astronomical Union (IAU). It assembles committees that express learned scientific points of view that occasionally blend with political will. To offend the fewest people (unlike what became of my *Natural History* essay), the IAU straddled the fence on the issue, allowing people to call Pluto a planet while simultaneously accepting the growing (and irreversible) movement to classify Pluto as a comet. In the meantime, I will continue to x-ray packages sent to my office from third graders.

Earth was not thought to be a planet for most of recorded history. Officially, planets were all those things that moved in the sky—there were seven of them, including the Sun and Moon. Earth was a unique, stationary object around which everything in the universe turned. The early pagan civilization of Mesopotamia believed that all objects in the heavens were gods, but the most powerful gods were the seven planets. These super-gods were ranked by their speed across the sky— the more slowly they moved, the more ancient and powerful they were. With Saturn the slowest and the Moon the fastest, the seven planets get ranked Saturn, Jupiter, Mars, Sun, Venus, Mercury, and the Moon. The Mesopotamians, and later the

Romans, assigned each planet to rule Earth's affairs in sequence, hour by hour, for every day. Whichever planet happened to rule the first hour of a twenty-four-hour day was that day's reigning planet.

An easy way to reconstruct the days of the week, in their familiar sequence, is to lay down a circle of the planets in sky-speed order:

**Saturn**

**Moon**                    **Jupiter**

**Mercury**                        **Mars**

**Venus**          **Sun**

Start anywhere around the circle (using the first spot as the first day) and count clockwise twenty-three more planets, one for each of the twenty-four hours in the "current" day. The twenty-fifth planet rules the next day. Restart your counting from one and continue this numerical ritual seven times in a row. You will recover all seven days of the week in calendar order: Saturn-day, Sun-day, Moon-day, Mars-day, Mercury-day, Jupiter-day, and Venus-day. When you substitute "Sabbath" for Saturday and "Lord's day" for Sunday, you get the basic Latin forms of the French, Italian, Spanish, and Portuguese names for the days of the week: Sabbata, Domenica, Luna, Martis, Mercurius, Jovis, Veneris. For some western languages (English included), substitute the Anglo-Saxon gods Tiu, Woden, Thor, and Frigga for their Roman counterparts to get to get Tuesday, Wednesday, Thursday, and Friday.

The prevalence of religious mythologies among scientifically ignorant cultures that flourished millennia ago makes it easy to see why they would believe that planet-gods exerted divine influence on human affairs. It's much harder to see why similar beliefs persist today, and every day, in the astrology pages of the newspapers, unless we admit to ourselves that contemporary society remains widely uninformed in matters of science. We fail in even the simplest of all scientific observations: Nobody looks up anymore. Why else would people be surprised to learn that the Moon also comes out in the daytime; that the North Star is not and was never in contention for being the brightest star in the nighttime sky; that for most of Earth's population the Sun has never appeared directly overhead at any time of day or on any day of the year; that most of the eighty-eight constellations in the sky are wholly unrecognizable patterns when compared with the creatures and objects that legends and mythologies declare them to be; and that the planets journey back and forth across the sky, from one side of the Sun to the next, getting brighter and dimmer and brighter again.

We live in the days of evening distractions that include television, multiplex cinemas, and even books that can be read by electric light after dark. When I was in graduate school at Columbia University in New York City, an elderly woman with a strong Brooklyn accent called my office to ask about a bright glowing object she saw "hovering" outside her window the night before. I knew that a few planets were bright and well placed for viewing in the early evening sky, but I asked more questions to verify my suspicions. After sifting through answers like, "It's a little bit higher than the roof of Marty's Deli," I concluded that the brightness, compass direction, elevation above the horizon, and time of observation were consistent with her having seen the planet Venus. Realizing that she has probably lived in Brooklyn most of her life, I asked her why she called then and not at any of the hundreds of other times that Venus was bright over the western horizon. She replied, "I've never noticed it before." You must understand that to an astrophysicist, this is an astonishing statement. I asked how long she has lived in her apartment. "Thirty years." I asked her whether she has ever looked out her window before. "I used to always keep my curtains closed, but now I keep them open." Naturally, I then asked her why she now keeps her curtains open. "There used to be a tall apartment building outside my window but they tore it down. Now I can see the sky and it's beautiful."

I have similar encounters with all sorts of people about once per month. When it's not Venus it's Jupiter or Mars. And when it's not planets, it's odd cloud formations or bright shooting stars. With phone calls such as these—people taking the time and energy to ask about what they do not understand—I have a renewed hope that society can shed its superstitions and embrace the enlightenment that comes from just a basic understanding of how the universe works.

The supply of professional astrophysicists in the world has held for some time at a steady ratio of one in a million people, which is not nearly enough. But it does mean that if you find yourself sitting next to an astrophysicist on the airplane then you had better ask all your pent-up questions about the universe. You do not know when your next encounter will be.

In addition to the current total of astrophysicists, we clearly need one astrophysicist for every disaster movie produced, and then some. With the nation's urban murder rates falling to half-century lows, the motion picture industry can no longer depict crime as a stereotype of life in the city. But unlike romantic comedies or action-adventure thrillers, most disaster films tap scientific arteries of knowledge for their story lines. Deadly viruses, out-of-control DNA, evil aliens, monsters, and killer meteors are recurring themes in apocalyptic films. Unfortunately, a film's scientific literacy hardly ever measures up to its plot, leading to unforgivable abuses of the way the world works.

I'm not talking about simple bloopers such as when a Roman centurion sports a wristwatch while riding a chariot. Or when the shadow of a microphone boom creeps into a scene. These mistakes are inadvertent. I'm talking about purposeful yet ignorant bloopers, like reversing the sunset to pretend you have filmed a sunrise. Are cinematographers too lazy to wake up before the Sun and get the real footage? Sunrise and sunset are not time-symmetric events.

Or how about when they show Christopher Columbus on the deck of the *Santa Maria*, peering though a telescope that would not be invented for another 116 years?

And why did James Cameron, the talented director of the 1997 film *Titanic*, take the time to get every imaginable detail correct—from the number of rivets in the hull, to the patterns in the dinner plates—yet he got the wrong nighttime sky? What might have been the constellation Corona Borealis (the northern crown) is shown overhead on that fateful night. But it has the wrong number of stars. Why? Had Cameron attended Camp Uraniborg this mistake might not have happened. I'd bet he researched the costumes to be precisely the styles of the period. If someone had been on board wearing love beads, bell-bottom jeans, and a large Afro, you know that viewers would have complained loudly that Cameron had not done his homework. Am I any less justified in my outcries?

My gripes are not just with Hollywood. What about those majestic stars in the ceiling of New York City's Grand Central Terminal? It's a canopy of constellations rising high above the heads of hurrying commuters who haven't got time to look up anyway. But the star patterns are backward when compared with the real night sky. Rather than just admitting the mistake, a sign in the lobby tells us, "Said to be backwards, [the ceiling is] actually seen from a point of view outside our solar system." But a second error has now been committed in an attempt to cover up the first: No point of view in our galaxy will reverse the constellation patterns of Earth's night sky. As you leave the solar system and travel among the stars, all that happens to Earth's constellations is that they become scrambled and wholly unrecognizable.

What society needs are scientifically literate reviewers. Why should a theater critic be limited to saying things like, "the characters stretched credulity," or "the tonal elements clashed with the emotional flavor of the set designs"? Just once I want to hear a critic say, "The Scarecrow botched his recital of the Pythagorean theorem when the Wizard gave him a diploma" when reviewing the 1939 fantasy classic *The Wizard of Oz*. A critic might also declare, "Flying saucers traveling quadrillions of miles through interstellar space don't need runway lights to land on Earth" when reviewing the 1977 almond-eyed alien classic *Close Encounters of the Third Kind*. I would have loved for a critic to notice that the Moon phases grew in the wrong direction throughout Steve Martin's otherwise charming 1991 romantic comedy *L.A. Story.* And I would have rejoiced had I heard just one critic say, "A killer asteroid the size of Texas would have been discovered two hundred years ago, not two weeks before impact" when reviewing the 1998 summer block-buster *Armageddon.*

Only when such errors are highlighted will the public begin to appreciate the inescapable role that the laws of physics play in everyday life.

If you want to write a book, make a film, or engage in a public art project, and if this work makes reference to the natural world, just call your neighborhood scientist and chat about it. When you seek "scientific license" to distort the laws of nature, or when you want to corrupt the appearance of night sky phenomena, then I prefer you did so knowing the truth, rather than inventing a story line cloaked in ignorance. You may be surprised to learn that valid science can make fertile additions to your storytelling—whether or not your artistic objective is to destroy the world.

Practically every scientific claim ever made was, or should have been, accompanied by a tandem measure of the reliability of the claim. When reporting scientific discoveries, the popular press hardly ever conveys these inherent uncertainties in the data or the interpretation. This seemingly innocent omission carries a subtle, misguided message: If it's a scientific study, the results are exact and correct. These same news reports often declare that scientists, having previously thought one thing, are now forced to think something else; or are forced to return to the mythic "drawing board" in a stupor. As a consequence, if you get all your science from press accounts then you might be led to believe that scientists arrogantly, yet aimlessly, bounce back and forth between one perceived truth and another without ever contributing to a base of objective knowledge.

But let's take a closer look.

New ideas put forth by well-trained research scientists will be wrong most of the time because the frontier of discovery is, for the most part, a messy place. But we know this and are further trained to quantify this level of ignorance with an estimate of the claim's uncertainty. The famous "plus-or-minus" sign is the most widely recognized example. We typically present a tentative result based on a shaky interpretation of poor data. Six months later, different yet equally bad data become available from somebody else's experiment and a different interpretation emerges. During this phase, which may drag on for years or even decades, news stories implying unassailable fact get written anyway.

Eventually, excellent data become available and a consensus emerges—a long-term process that does not lend itself to late-breaking news reports. Studies on environmental health risks, or the effects of food consumption on diseases and longevity, are especially susceptible to being overinterpreted. The financial consequences of premature news stories, and the attendant reactions on Wall Street, can be staggering. In 1992 a Florida man brought a lawsuit against two cellular phone manufacturers by claiming that his wife's death from brain cancer was caused by her heavy use of cellular phones. When this and several similar claims hit the news in late January 1993, the market capitalization of publicly traded cellular phone companies fell by billions of dollars in less than a week. I had several astrophysics colleagues who were financially poised to take advantage of this lemminglike market reaction to the perceived hazards of cell phones. A little bit of analysis goes far: You can get brain cancer without ever using a cellular phone. And since the popularity of cellular phones was on the rise, you would expect some users to die from brain cancer just as some users would die from heart disease, or from old age. In this case there was no definitive study to establish a cause and effect between cellular phone use and brain cancer, yet people overreacted anyway. Fortunately, most of the comings and goings of astrophysics have so little impact on how people conduct their daily lives that I can spend more time joking about the problem than crying about it.

Initial uncertainty is a natural element of the scientific method, yet the scientific method is, without question, the most powerful and successful path ever devised to understand the physical world. When a published scientific finding is confirmed and reconfirmed and re-reconfirmed and re-re-reconfirmed, then further confirmation becomes less interesting than working on another problem. At that time, and only at that time, the new nuggets of knowledge are justifiably presented with little or no uncertainty in the basic textbooks of the day. Consistency and repeatability are the hallmarks of a genuine scientific finding. For if the laws of physics and chemistry were different from lab to lab, and from one moment to the next, then scientists would all just pack up and go home.

In person, scientists have been known to completely ignore

their uncertainties because, for the most part, scientists are people too. There are arrogant ones, lovable ones, loud ones, soft-spoken ones, and bone-headed ones. Every scientist, myself included, has colleagues who fill each category. In published research papers, however, we are typically timid because of the semipermanence of the printed word and because of the overwhelming frequency of wrong ideas. Most results flow from the edge of our understanding and are therefore subject to large uncertainties.

More often than not, a scientist's printed word presents an honest, almost humble uncertainty that goes unnoticed when people reflect on the history of scientific misconceptions. What about that 1996 research paper that claimed to have found life in a Martian meteorite? Writing in the journal *Science*, the nine coauthors noted, among other things, in their abstract:

> *The carbonate globules [in the Martian meteorite]*
> *are similar in texture and size to some terrestrial*
> *bacterially induced carbonate precipitates.*
> *Although inorganic formation is possible, forma-*
> *tion of the globules by biogenic processes could ex-*
> *plain many of the observed features . . . and could*
> *thus be fossil remains of past Martian biota.*

From the oversize newspaper headlines that followed and the persistent media requests for my time, you would never guess that the original research paper contained such unassertive language.

A rare but now-famous case of misreported uncertainty coupled with an overconfident claim by a scientist took place in early 1998, when the Central Bureau for Astronomical Telegrams (the clearinghouse for astronomers of the world who need to disseminate up-to-the-minute sky phenomena among colleagues) announced the discovery of a mile-wide asteroid whose orbit would bring it dangerously close to Earth in the year 2028. (Formerly sent around the world via telegram, these notices are now distributed instantly via e-mail.) The offending asteroid was coded 1997 XF11, which cryptically identifies when in the year 1997 the asteroid was discovered. This was the asteroid that prompted the infamous "Nice tie" remark from Peter Jennings on ABC's *World News Tonight*. The telegram reported on March 11, 1998:

> *This object, discovered by J. V. Scotti in the course of the Spacewatch program at the University of Arizona on 1997 Dec. 6 . . . recognized as one of the 108 "potentially hazardous asteroids," has been under observation through 1998 Mar. 4 . . . An orbit computation from the 88-day arc . . . indicates that the object will pass only 0.00031 AU from the earth on 2028 Oct. 26.73 UT! Error estimates suggest that passage within 0.002 AU is virtually certain, this figure being decidedly smaller than has been reliably predicted for generally fainter potentially hazardous asteroids in the foreseeable future.*

When converted to everyday language, the announcement declared that the asteroid's most likely path would bring it within thirty thousand miles of Earth, but the uncertainty in the calculation allowed the asteroid to come anywhere within a two-hundred-thousand-mile "error-circle" surrounding Earth.

I remember reading this telegram from my office at Princeton University within hours after its release. All I could think to myself was: It was bound to happen some time. In the year 2028 I will be seventy years old. What a way to go! Put me at ground zero for the impact. But then I recoiled from an unfamiliar combination of emotions: one of shock, that life as we know it could end in my natural lifetime, and one of perverse pride in knowing the laws of physics that enabled us to make the prediction.

When the substance of the telegram was further distributed via press release from the American Astronomical Society, passing along the hair-raising words "virtually certain," a media deluge followed.

The telegram went on to give the best available coordinates for the object—obtained from observers who were tracking it—preceded by a scientifically sensible appeal: "The following ephemeris is given in the hope that further observations will allow refinement of the 2028 miss distance." The next day, on March 12, 1998, another telegram appeared that announced the existence of what astronomers call a "prediscovery" photograph of the asteroid, obtained from archival survey images taken in 1990. This significantly extended the baseline of observations to well beyond the original eighty-eight days. (Longer baselines always provide more accurate estimates than shorter ones.) Calculations that incorporated the new data narrowed the error-circle to a skinny ellipse that handily shifted Earth from within the range of collision uncertainty to well outside of it. Five weeks later, a telegram was issued that corrected the alarmist language of the first announcement and admitted that the original telegram's uncertainties could have been sharpened if a more sophisticated method of calculation had been used.

The episode was widely reported as a blunder, but at worst, the original calculation was simply incomplete. At best, it was a valid scientific starting point. True, the survival of the human species was involved, but most important, everything worked the way it was supposed to. The early estimate, and the better estimates that followed (within a day!) were a model of the scientific method and how it has the power to refine itself as our knowledge approaches an objective reality.

After what had been twenty-four hours of sensationalist journalism across the country, the retraction spawned sighs of relief. In particular, the *New York Post*, a colorfully written daily newspaper in New York City, ran the inimitable headline: "KISS YOUR ASTEROID GOODBYE." And a few days later, an illustration by cartoonist Jesse Gordon on the Op Ed page of the *New York Times* depicted the asteroid changing its collision course over a sequence of panels. We are treated to the top nine reasons why the asteroid has decided not to hit Earth, one of them being "No desire to spend the rest of its days in the lobby of the Museum of Natural History."

How certain can we be of a scientific measurement? Confirmation matters. Only rarely is the importance of this fact captured in the media or the movies. The 1997 film *Contact*, based on the 1983 novel of the same name by the celebrated astronomer Carl Sagan, was an exception. It portrayed what might happen—scientifically, socially, and politically—if one day we make radio-wave contact with extraterrestrial intelligence. When a radio signal from the star Vega rises above the din of cosmic noise, Jodie Foster (who plays an astrophysicist) alerts colleagues in Australia, who could observe the signal long after the stars in that region of the sky had set for Americans. Only when the Australians confirm her measurements does she go public with the discovery. Her original signal might have been a systematic glitch in the telescope's electronics. It might have been a local prankster beaming signals into the telescope from across the street. It might have been a local collective delusion. Her confidence was boosted only when somebody else on another telescope with different electronics driving an independent computer system got the same results.

The accuracy and integrity of the above scene almost make up for a grave mathematical blunder earlier in the film. In a scene where Jodie Foster and her handsome love interest, Matthew McConaughey, take their first kiss, Jodie Foster recites the following line:

> *If there are 400 billion stars in our galaxy, and only one in a million of them had planets, and only one in a million of those stars with planets had life, and only one in a million of the stars with planets that have life, have intelligent life, that still leaves millions of planets to explore.*

If you do the arithmetic correctly, you are left with not "millions" of planets but 0.0000004 planets to explore. For this blunder I don't blame the writers or producers. They have enough on their minds.

I blame Jodie Foster.

She must have rehearsed her lines many times over. There must have been multiple takes of the same scene, as is common in high-budget films. At some point she might have caught the error. Last I checked, she was a graduate of Yale. I'm pretty sure they teach arithmetic there.

I was one of the lucky few to attend the world premiere of *Contact* in Pasadena, California, by the invitation of Ann Druyan, Sagan's widow and coauthor of the film's story. It was my first and only Hollywood world premiere. In attendance was also the astrophysicist Frank Drake, whose famous Drake Equation was the subject of Jodie Foster's numerical recitation. During the infamous scene, Frank Drake did not convulse and was remarkably forgiving in his attitude and behavior, so I could not justify taking any more action than he did, which was nothing.

If Americans had more training with the metric system and powers of ten in general, then the relationship between and among numerical quantities would become a matter of understanding rather than of rote memory. Compare the following sentence pairs: A *kilo*meter is 1,000 meters, a mile is 5,280 feet. A meter is 100 *centi*meters, a yard is 36 inches. A liter contains 10 *deci*liters, a quart contains 32 ounces. With powers of ten built into the metric system of measurement, had Jodie Foster been comfortable with it she might have calculated what was going on in her lines rather than simply memorized them.

The system of royal governance was not the only thing overthrown during the French Revolution of 1789. So too was the system of weights and measures that was based on the length of various human body parts and on arcane references to nonstandardized containers. What replaced it was the decimal system, inspired by the fact that the average person has ten fingers and ten toes, which led to a counting system that uses ten numerals. If our species naturally had some other number of fingers we surely would be using a different counting system. I have no doubt that octopuses and arachnids do their arithmetic in base eight.

Today anybody who needs to know the metric system knows it. This includes scientists, engineers, and international industrial corporations. Only four countries are left in the world that do not officially sanction the metric system in their general population: Liberia, Burma, South Yemen, and the United States of America. America, the largest military, economic, and industrial force the world has ever seen, commonly uses inches, feet, and miles, and pints, quarts, and gallons for its daily measurements. A government initiative to convert Americans over to the metric system, begun in the 1970s, has largely failed. It's the sort of thing you need to accomplish cold turkey. Maps, road signs, and even baseball parks all posted dual distances that included the metric system, which meant nobody had to learn a thing. For its metric transgressions, America lost a $125 million Mars orbiting spacecraft in 1999 because the engineers reported thrust in the English units of "pounds," while the scientists assumed it had been reported in the metric units of "newtons." The spacecraft failed to achieve the correct speed for a Martian orbit and was promptly lost, presumed crashed on the surface. This class of failure is common when you initiate a changeover program and abandon it halfway.

I don't think that the Fahrenheit temperature scale will ever lose ground to Celsius in America. As arcane and logic-defying as the Fahrenheit scale is, its ten-degree increments are too useful for weather forecasters to abandon: Simple proclamations such as "It'll be in the sixties today" or "The temperature will drop down into the teens tonight" or "The temperature will stay in the nineties today" have served to group temperature intervals into comfort levels. But other aspects of the scale, such as its low and unfamiliar zero point, have left some Americans hopelessly confused. A few years ago, I happened to be listening to the radio in midwinter when the outdoor Fahrenheit temperature was in the low single digits. In New York City, temperatures that low are sufficiently rare to warrant fresh observations on the meaning and significance of air that cold. The temperature dropped slowly through the night, degree by degree. As the readings neared zero, the announcer declared with what was surely a straight face, "There is almost no temperature left."

In spite of isolated embarrassing moments such as those, I am happy to support our colloquial vocabulary, born of the British system of units: Motion picture cameras will not stop shooting *footage* of film. *Mile*stones in people's lives won't all of a sudden go away. Running backs in American football will continue to gain (or lose) *yardage* on the gridiron. Car owners will never abandon the *mileage* measure of an engine's efficiency. We will surely not give up the use of *inch* as a verb. *Inchworms* should be environmentally protected from going metric. Small people will continue to be *pint*-size. And an *ounce* of prevention will forever provide a *pound* of cure.

Unlike most of my colleagues, I am neither upset nor concerned that America is not entirely metric. One of my reasons is that America is largely metric already, although people don't realize it. Our money has 100 pennies to the dollar. Our standard photographic film is 35 millimeters. The size of camera lenses, and filters that screw into them, are all measured in millimeters, as is the size of binoculars. All wine bottles and most liquor bottles are 750 milliliters and multiples (or fractions) of it. Piston displacement for car engines is now routinely measured in liters. One-and three-liter plastic bottles of soft drinks are industry standards. Nine-millimeter pistols are becoming the handgun of choice for urban law enforcement. The brightness of household lightbulbs and the power of hair dryers are both measured in watts, a metric unit of energy consumption. The power of a car battery is measured in volts and amps, each a metric unit of electricity. Nearly all races run by athletes are measured in round-number meter-length distances. All prescription and over-the-counter medicines have the strength of their active ingredients measured in grams. And kilos are, of course, a standard unit of drug trafficking.

My primary reason for not caring whether America goes metric is that the British system of feet and Fahrenheit, acres and inches, and pints and pounds, carries some charming history, even if people who use the terms do not know it. When you are a visitor to America, our units of measure become one of the things telling you that you have landed in a country different from your own—a country with different history and different customs.

As a visitor to America, the absence of the metric system will, of course, be the least of your adjustment problems. The hodge-podge collection of words that comprise American

English, along with paper money that is all the same size and color, might be a greater concern than whether you can interpret the Fahrenheit temperature on a flashing bank thermometer. When you visit another country you expect things to be different. That's the most common reason why people go on vacation—to be someplace different. As long as baseball fields are measured in yards, hotdogs come in packs of eight to the pound, and the ingredients to grandma's apple pie are measured in cups and teaspoons, you know you are in America— land of the free and of the metrically challenged.

# THREE

# DARK MATTERS

A VIEW FROM THE DARK SIDE OF SPACE

THERE'S NO WAY TO PUT IT GENTLY. The twentieth century ended without our knowing what causes 90 percent of the gravity in the universe. What we call "dark matter" emits no light in any form and does not interact with ordinary (household) matter by any known means. Its identity remains a mystery, although its gravity is immediately apparent. In an example from our home galaxy, the outer regions of our Milky Way revolve around the galactic center ten times faster than they otherwise would, were it not for the actions of dark matter. Ordinary matter and dark matter coexist, not in parallel universes, but side by side in the same universe. They feel each other's gravity but otherwise do not respond to each other's presence.

Perhaps astrophysicists are at the dawn of a new era of scientific discovery, just as the physicists were in 1900. At the

time, various loose threads in prevailing theories began to un-
ravel. They eventually unraveled completely, opening the door
to entirely new branches of physics. One of them, called quantum mechanics, accurately accounts for Nature's behavior on
its smallest scales—molecules, atoms, and particles. Nearly a
dozen Nobel prizes were awarded to the scientific leaders of
that effort.

Dark matter may be an assortment of exotic subatomic
particles, as some theories have proposed. But it may be something yet to be imagined. The dark matter dilemma in astrophysics at the dawn of the twenty-first century may force a
revolution in our understanding of gravity and (or) matter that
rivals the scientific revolutions of the past.

Occasionally, I cannot help but personalize, even personify,
dark matter's place in the universe. Especially the part about
matter and dark matter feeling each other's gravity but not otherwise interacting. During the summer of 1991, I attended an
annual conference of one of the national physics societies of
which I am a member, near Atlanta, Georgia. That fall I would
begin my postdoctoral appointment at Princeton. At such conferences, physicists gather from across the country, leaving
their academic hamlets, their industrial labs, their particle ac-
celerators, and their government installations to share the
latest, yet-to-be-published results on the frontier of human understanding of the universe. During the prescheduled coffee
breaks in the lounge areas of these outsize hotels, people engage in intense discussions about that day's presentations.

There is something truly comforting at physics conferences.
They are places where you feel as if you know people who
you have never met before, simply because everyone's life

path strongly resembles your own. Surely this is true for all conferences, no matter the field. Among professional physicists, for example, we all got good grades in school (physicists are disproportionately represented among college seniors who graduate magna and summa cum laude). We have all solved the same homework problems in physics classes. We have all read the same books. We wield nearly identical vocabulary sets when describing the physical world. And we have all felt the occasional aspersions cast by pop society on our intellectual abilities.

By the time of the society banquet, held the last night of the conference, people have loosened their collars and discussions are more likely to touch upon things that have nothing to do with the subjects and themes of the conference. By the end of this particular banquet, a dozen of us from several adjacent tables collected the unfinished bottles of wine and retreated to one of those penthouse common rooms on the top floor of the hotel. We talked (and argued) about what the rest of society would surely consider to be geeky and pointless, such as why a can of Diet Pepsi floats while a can of regular Pepsi sinks. That was a new one to me, although I did have latent memories from the end of long parties where all the ice had melted in the beverage cooler and some soft drinks were floating while others were resting at the bottom.

We lamented the fact that the transporter in the television and film series *Star Trek* does not transport perfectly across space. Apparently the teleported copy sustains an extremely small but quantifiable level of degradation when compared with the original—a perversely humorous fact that was well known among the *Star Trek* cognoscenti. The questions to be debated started rolling: How many times could you be transported back and forth between the starship and a planet before you started to look different? What part of your body would change? Was it your DNA? Was it your atomic structure? Or would you one day beam back to the ship without a nose?

We also debated the popularity of the physicist Stephen Hawking, who is known to the public primarily through his best-selling book on the state and fate of the universe, *A Brief History of Time*. Some felt that he has been overrated as a scientist by the public as well as by other scientists. We all agreed that he is a pretty smart guy, and that he is an excellent physicist. But we further agreed that he falls below a dozen other physicists from the twentieth century, most of whom the public has never heard of. We bandied about a short list, including: Bohr, de Broglie, Dirac, Eddington, Fermi, Friedmann, Gamow, Gell-Mann, Heisenberg, and Planck. One of my colleagues, a theoretical physicist whose expertise overlaps with that of Hawking, spent some time detailing all the theories that Hawking got wrong. Yes, physicists can be petty and gossipy too.

The evening was rich in the expression of applied mental energy. What else could you have expected among intellectual soul mates, at the end of a full meal, near the end of a full conference, while sipping good wine into the late evening?

Around midnight, during our discussion on momentum transfer in car accidents, one of us mentioned a time when the police stopped him while driving his car. They ordered him from his sports car and conducted a thorough search of his body, the car seats and the trunk before sending him on his way with a hefty ticket. The charge for stopping him? Driving twenty miles per hour over the local speed limit. Try as we did, we could not muster sympathy for his case, although a brief discussion of the precision of police radar guns followed. We all agreed that on a straight road, radar guns cannot possibly register your exact speed unless the police officer stands in the middle of the oncoming traffic. If the officer stands anywhere else, the measured speed will be less than your actual speed. So if you were measured to be speeding, you were speeding.

My colleague had other encounters with the law that he shared later that night, but his first started a chain reaction among us. One by one we each recalled multiple incidents of being stopped by the police. None of the accounts were particularly violent or life-threatening, although it was easy to extrapolate to highly publicized cases that were. One of my colleagues had been stopped for driving too slowly. He was admiring the local flora as he drove through a New England town in the autumn. Another colleague had been stopped because he was speeding, but only by five miles per hour. He was questioned and then released without getting a ticket. Still another colleague had been stopped and questioned for jogging down the street late at night.

As for me, I had a dozen different encounters to draw from. There was the time I was stopped late at night at an underpass on an empty road in New Jersey for having changed lanes without signaling. The officer told me to get out of my car and questioned me for ten minutes around back with the headlights of his squad car brightly illuminating my face. Is this your car? Yes. Who is the woman in the passenger seat? My wife. Where are you coming from? My parents' house. Where are you going? Home. What do you do for a living? I am an astrophysicist at Princeton University. What's in your trunk? A spare tire, and a lot of other greasy junk. He went on to say that the "real reason" he stopped me was because my car's license plates were much newer and shinier than the seventeen-year-old Ford that I was driving. The officer was just making sure that neither the car nor the plates were stolen.

In my other stories, I had been stopped by the police while transporting my home supply of physics textbooks into my newly assigned office in graduate school. They had stopped me at the entrance to the physics building, where they asked accusatory questions about what I was doing. This one was complicated because a friend offered to drive me and my boxes to my office (I had not yet learned to drive). Her car was registered in her father's name. It was 11:30 P.M. Open-topped boxes of graduate math and physics textbooks filled the trunk. And we were transporting them into the building. I wonder how often that scenario shows up in police training tapes.

In that conference hotel room, we exchanged stories about the police for two more hours before retiring to our respective hotel rooms. Being mathematically literate, of course, we looked for "common denominators" among the stories. But we had all driven different cars—some were old, others were new, some were undistinguished, others were high-performance imports. Some police stops were in the daytime, others were at night. Taken one by one, each encounter with the law could be explained as an isolated incident where, in modern times, we all must forfeit some freedoms to ensure a safer society for us all. Taken collectively, however, you would think the cops resented physicists because our profession was the only profile we all had in common. One thing was for sure: Our stories were not singular, novel moments playfully recounted. They were common, recurring episodes. How could this assembly of highly educated scientists, each in possession of the Ph.D.—the highest academic degree in the land—be so vulnerable to police inquiry in their lives?

Maybe the police cued on something else. Maybe it was the color of our skin. The conference I had been attending was the twenty-third annual meeting of the National Society of Black Physicists. We were guilty not of DWI (Driving While Intoxicated) but of other violations none of us knew were on the books: DWB (Driving While Black), WWB (Walking While Black), and of course, JBB (Just Being Black).

A year after the conference, Rodney King was pulled from his car by the Los Angeles Police and, while handcuffed, "tasered," and lying facedown on the street, was beaten senseless with nightsticks. What sometimes goes unremembered is that the deadly riots that followed in South Central L.A. were not triggered by the beating itself but by the subsequent acquittal in the court of law of key participating officers. Upon seeing the now-famous videotape of the incident, I remembered being surprised not because Rodney King was beaten by the police but because somebody finally caught such an incident on tape.

The next meeting of the National Society of Black Physicists, held in Jackson, Mississippi, happened to coincide with those Los Angeles riots. I was scheduled to give the luncheon keynote address on May 1, 1992, on the success or failure of undergraduate physics education in the academic pipeline that leads to the Ph.D. While watching the helicopter news coverage of the fires and violence of that morning, I had a surreal revelation: The news headlines were dominated by Black people rioting and not by Black physicists presenting their latest research on the nature of the universe. Of course, by most measures of news priorities, urban riots trump everything else, so I was not surprised. I was simply struck by this juxtaposition of events, which led me to abandon my original keynote address and replace it with ten minutes of reflective observations on NSBP's immeasurable significance to the perception of Blacks by Whites in America. My comments included the brief reminiscence of a college turning point of my life.

During the spring of my sophomore year at Harvard, I was well into the course work of my field of concentration, taking an (un)healthy dose of physics and math classes as well as the requisite other nonscience courses that a full schedule requires. That year I also wrestled for the university team, as second-string to a more talented senior in my 190-pound weight category. One day after practice, we were walking out of the athletic facility when he asked me what I had been up to lately. I replied, "My math and physics problem sets are taking nearly all of my time. And I barely have time to sleep or go to the bathroom." Then he asked me what my academic major was. When I told him physics, with a special interest in astrophysics, he paused for a moment, waved his hand in front of my chest, and declared, "Blacks in America do not have the luxury of your intellectual talents being spent on astrophysics."

No wrestling move he had ever put on me was as devastating as those accusatory words. Never before had anyone so casually, yet so succinctly, indicted my life's ambitions.

My wrestling buddy was an economics major, and a month earlier, had been awarded the Rhodes Scholarship to Oxford where, upon graduation, he planned to study innovative economic solutions to assist impoverished urban communities. I knew in my mind that I was doing the right thing with my life (whatever the "right thing" meant), but I knew in my heart that he was right. And until I could resolve this inner conflict, I would forever carry a level of surpressed guilt for pursuing my esoteric interests in the universe.

During graduation week of my senior year of college, an article appeared in the *New York Times* that broadly profiled the 131 Black graduates of my Harvard class of 1,600 people. The *Times* made public for the first time that only 2 of the 131 graduates had plans to continue for advanced academic degrees. I was one of those two. The rest were slated for law school, medical school, business school, or self-employment. (The other "academic" happened to be a friend of mine from the Bronx High School of Science who graduated from college in four years with both his bachelor's and master's degrees in history.) Given these data I became further isolated from the brilliant good-deed doers of my generation.

Nine years passed. Having earned my master's degree from the University of Texas at Austin, I spent several more years there before leaving to teach for a year at the University of Maryland and finally transferring my doctoral program to Columbia University. At Columbia I was well on my way to completing the Ph.D. in astrophysics when I received a phone call at my office from the local affiliate of Fox News. I had already been the department's unofficial contact for public and media inquiries about sky phenomena, so this call was not itself unusual—except that it would change my life.

Several explosions on the Sun had been identified by a recently launched solar satellite, and the Fox News desk wanted to know if everything would be okay in the solar system. After I offered my assurances that we would all survive the incident, they invited me to appear in a pretaped interview to convey this information for that evening's broadcast. When I agreed, they sent a car to pick me up. Graduate students are generally not known for fashion or neatness, and I was no exception. Between the phone call and when the car arrived I ran home, shaved, and put on a jacket and tie. At the television station I was interviewed by their weatherman in a comfortable chair in front of a bookshelf filled with fake, sawed-off books. The interview lasted two minutes, within which I said that explosions on the Sun happen all the time, but especially on eleven-year cycles during "solar maximum" when the Sun's surface is more turbulent than usual. During these times, high doses of charged subatomic particles spew forth from the Sun and fly through interplanetary space. Those particles that head toward Earth deflect toward the poles by the action of Earth's magnetic field. Subsequent collisions of these particles with molecules in Earth's upper atmosphere create a dancing curtain of colors, visible primarily in the arctic regions. These are the famous Northern (and Southern) lights. I assured the viewers that Earth's atmosphere and magnetic field protects us from these hazards and that people might as well take the opportunity to travel north in search of these displays.

The interview took place at 3:00 P.M. and was scheduled to air during their six o'clock news. I promptly called everybody I knew and rushed home to watch.

That evening, while I was eating dinner, the segment aired.

In the middle of my mashed potatoes, I had an intellectual out-of-body experience: On the screen before me was a scientific expert on the Sun whose knowledge was sought by the evening news. The expert on television happened to be Black. At that moment, the entire fifty-year history of television programming flew past my view. At no place along that time line could I recall a Black person (who is neither an entertainer nor an athlete) being interviewed as an expert on something that had nothing whatever to do with being Black. Of course there had been (and continued to be) Black experts on television, but they were politicians seeking support and monies for urban programs to help Blacks in the ghetto. They were Black preachers and other clergy offering spiritual leadership. They were Black sociologists analyzing crime and homelessness in the Black community. They were Black business executives talking about enterprise zones in the most impoverished regions of town. And they were Black journalists, writing about Black issues.

For the first time in nine years I stood without guilt for following my cosmic dreams. I realized as clear as the crystalline spheres of antiquity that one of the major barriers to successful relations between Blacks and Whites is the latent supposition that Blacks as a group are just not as smart as Whites. This notion runs deep—very deep. It's fed in part by differences in IQ scores and in other standardized exams such as the SATs, where Whites on average score higher than Blacks. Its influence is felt in debates on academic tracking, affirmative action (in schools and the workplace), and the international politics of Africa. The most pervasive expression of the problem is the casually dismissive manner in which many Whites treat Blacks in society.

I have never had an IQ exam, which is possible in this world if you attend only public instead of private schools. I nonetheless know all about them and what they look like from reading extensively on the subject. Among the claims of IQ proponents is that the single number, your intelligence quotient, is largely inbred and is an indicator of your innate intelligence and your likelihood of succeeding in life. Data show that Blacks, on average, score a full standard deviation lower than Whites. The prevailing notion is that you cannot substantially increase your IQ at any time, so one might conclude that Whites are genetically higher scorers, independent of upbringing, accumulated wealth, or birthright opportunities.

Since humans can get better and better in everything else that matters in the world simply by practicing, I have a ways questioned the relevance of the IQ exam to one's promise and performance in life. If one's ability to succeed were strongly dependent on a heritable IQ, then why do some Whites fear integrated schools? Why the high anxiety and the intense competition that surrounds school choice, from prekindergarten through college? Why the heavy monetary investment in education among those who can afford it? This collective behavior betrays a deep notion that wealth and choice of schools, not IQ, are the most significant factors influencing one's chances of success in life.

Since the words "smart" and "genius" get applied to scientists far more often than to people in other professions, this most fundamental barrier in "race relations" has yet to be crossed. Indeed, the barrier's true nature has yet to be identified.

The incentive to achieve knows no bounds. My father, when in high school, was singled out in his gym class by the instructor as having a body type that would not perform well in track events. My father's muscular build did not fit the lean stereotype of a runner that the instructor had formulated. My father had never run before. But almost out of spite, he went on to become a world-class track star in the 1940s and 1950s—at one time capturing the fifth fastest time in the world for the six-hundred-yard run. After college, my father continued to run for the New York Pioneer Club, an amateur track organization whose doors were open to Blacks and Jews and anybody else who was denied admission to the WASP-only athletic clubs. One of my father's longtime friends and Pioneer Club buddies once competed in a race where he was barely ahead of the number two runner as they approached the final straightaway. At that moment, the coach of the other runner loudly yelled, "Catch that nigger!" In the world of epithetic utterances, this one ranks among the least intelligent. My father's friend, having overheard the command, declared to himself, "This is one nigger he ain't going to catch" and won the race by an even larger margin.

An academic counterpart to the phrase "Catch that nigger" may be found in my growing collection of scholarly books over the centuries that assert the inferiority of Blacks. One of my favorites comes from the 1870 study *Hereditary Genius: An Inquiry into its Laws and Consequences,* by the English sociobiologist Francis Galton, founder of the eugenics movement. In the chapter titled "The Comparative Worth of Different Races" he notes:

> *The number among the negroes of those whom we should call half-witted men, is very large. Every book alluding to Negro Servants in America is full of instances. I was myself much impressed by this fact during my travels in Africa. The mistakes the negroes made in their own matters, which were so childish, stupid, and simpleton-like, as frequently to make me ashamed of my own species\**

Whenever I need energy to fight the pressures of society, I just reread one of these passages and, like my father's track buddy, I instantly summon the energy within me to ascend whatever mountain lies before me.

By winning four gold medals and four world records in track and field, Jesse Owens wiped the slate clean of Aryan claims to physical superiority during the 1936 Berlin Olympics. So too will a Black American Nobel laureate (in a category other than peace) forever change the dialogue on innate intellectual differences. Who knows when that time will come. In the interim, I play my small part in this journey. I've been interviewed on national television sixty times over the past six years for my expertise on all aspects of modern astrophysics—from discoveries in the solar system to theories of the early universe. And I have refused all invitations to speak for Black

---

\*1870, Francis Galton, *Hereditary Genius: An inquiry into its Laws and Consequences,* (D. Appleton & Co., New York) p. 339.

history month on the premise that my expertise is neither seasonal nor occasional.

I had finally reconciled my decade of inner conflict borne of a flippant comment by my fellow wrestler. It's not that the plight of the Black community cannot afford having me study astrophysics. It's that the plight of the Black community cannot afford it if I don't.

My life's goal from the age of nine had always been the Ph.D. in astrophysics. When I finally achieved it, I was determined to share what I had been through. The right moment arrived when I had the honor of addressing my fellow doctoral candidates in all disciplines from anthropology to zoology at Columbia University's Ph.D. graduation ceremony.

When the dean had first asked me to speak, it occurred to me that I had nothing to say. I could chat about my research, but the audience wouldn't understand the contents of my dissertation any more than I would understand the contents of theirs if it was they who were talking to me. I could expound upon the role of high-level academia in modern society, but you could get that at any convocation or commencement.

My inspiration for the address came from a mountaintop in the Andes Mountains in Chile, where I lived nocturnally for seven days. The trip's purpose was to obtain data on the structure of the Milky Way galaxy from a location seven thousand feet above sea level at the telescopes of the Cerro Tololo Inter-American Observatory, fifty kilometers from the nearest town. It is there that I obtained nearly all my thesis data, and it is there that I reflected upon my life's path through time and space.

When I was in elementary school in the public schools of New York City, I distinctly remember that it was important for me to be athletic—in particular, to be able to run fast. I was encouraged by all around me. My reward was the respect and admiration of classmates and especially my streetmates.

In junior high school it was important for me, now that I was certified the "fastest on the block," to slam-dunk a basketball. To do this you have to jump high *and* palm the basketball. On April 17, 1973, I was the first in my grade to slam-dunk a basketball. I then asked myself, "Is this all there is to it?" The answer is basically yes, yet one can imagine creative variations such as a 360-degree pirouette in midair preceding the dunk, but you still only score 2 points.

About the same time, I learned that light, traveling at 186,282 miles per second, moves too slowly to escape from the event horizon of a black hole. This was more astonishing to me than a 360-degree slam-dunk. I soon became scientifically curious and read everything I could find about the universe. I began to see myself as a future scientist—in particular, an astrophysicist. It became a deeply seated dream.

I shortly came to the shattering awareness that few parts of society were prepared to accept my dreams. I wanted to do with my life what people of my skin color were not supposed to do. As an athlete, I did not violate society's expectations since there was adequate precedent for dark-skinned competitors in the Olympics and in professional sports. To be an astrophysicist, however, became a "path of most resistance." I began to wonder whether I originally wanted to be an athlete more from society's interest rather than my own.

In high school, nobody probed further about how I became

captain of the wrestling team. But when I became editor in chief of my school's annual *Physical Science Journal*, my qualifications were constantly queried. And when I was accepted to the college of my choice, I was continually asked for my SAT scores and grade-point average. Indeed, one fellow student, who worked in the office of the guidance counselor, threatened to find the file in the school records to read my scores himself, if I didn't tell.

When I first entered graduate school, before coming to Columbia, I was eager to pursue my dreams of research astrophysics. But the first comment directed to me in the first minute of the first day, by a faculty member who I had just met was, "You must join our department basketball team." As the months and years passed, faculty and fellow students would suggest alternative careers for me thinking that they were doing me a favor:

> *"Why don't you become a computer salesman?"*
> *"Why don't you teach at a community college?"*
> *"Why don't you leave astrophysics and academia?*
>   *You can make much more money in industry."*

At no time was I perceived as a future colleague, although this privilege was enjoyed by others in graduate school.

When combined with the dozens of times I have been stopped and questioned by the police for going to and from my office after hours, and the hundreds of times I am followed by security guards in department stores, and the countless times people cross the street upon seeing me approach them on the sidewalk, I can summarize my life's path by noting that in the perception of society: My athletic talents are genetic; I am a likely mugger-rapist; my academic failures are expected; and my academic successes are attributed to others.

To spend most of my life fighting these attitudes levies an emotional tax that constitutes a form of intellectual emasculation. When the Ph.D. was conferred on me in 1991, it brought the national total of Black astrophysicists from six to seven (out of four thousand nationwide). Given what I experienced, I am surprised that many survived.

I eventually learned that you can be ridden only if your back is bent. And, of course, that which doesn't kill you makes you stronger. When I finally transferred my graduate program to Columbia University, where I was welcomed by the Department of Astronomy, I received a twice-renewed NASA research fellowship, published four research papers, attended four international conferences, had two popular-level books published, was quoted three times in the *New York Times*, appeared twice on network television, and was appointed to a well-respected postdoctoral research position at Princeton University's Department of Astrophysical Sciences.

There are no limits when you are surrounded by people who believe in you; people whose expectations are not set by the shortsighted attitudes of society—people who help to open doors of opportunity, not close them.

A common question on my applications to attend college was "What are your goals?" My response was simply, "A Ph.D. in astrophysics," a goal that had been planted within me when I was nine years old. With the conferral of my Columbia Ph.D.

that day, I had fulfilled my dream, yet I knew my life had just begun and that my struggle would continue.

I was once a family guest at a hilltop wedding reception for my sister-in-law in the farmlands of Washington state. Attending was the usual complement of extended family as well as some neighborhood friends. At dusk on this windless day, as part of the celebration a small, low-flying crop duster approached the hill and emptied bushels of popcorn all over the grass where we were gathered. The corn descended in slow motion, like wind-blown dandelion seeds. While I was eating the ceremonial corn off the ground (and off people's heads), I wondered to myself whether the popcorn had fallen straight down, or whether it landed forward or backward from the spot where it was released from the airplane. From the point of view of the pilot, of course, all popcorn moves immediately backward from its release point. My question, however, was intended from the point of view of someone standing on the ground.

Fully popped corn has such high air resistance that one might expect it to lose its airplane speed immediately and fall straight to the ground. But the rearward moving air from the propeller blades might have thrown it backward from its actual drop point in spite of the forward speed of the aircraft. Since I didn't immediately figure out the answer, I decided to ask the question of one of the guests, who was alone and quietly sipping champagne. I think he was an instructor at the local university. Upon hearing my question, he instantly assumed I was ignorant of all matters scientific and described, in a patronizing tone, how the low density of popcorn allows it to encounter very high air resistance upon being released from the airplane. Of course I already knew this. My query had been more subtle. I said to him, "I am not convinced that the corn will have no reverse motion after it is dropped. The wash from the propeller may send it backward."

He proceeded to pick up a popped kernel of corn from the grass and impatiently dropped it from his hand to demonstrate his point, as though I were the one in the conversation who was dense. He was surely oblivious to the fact that our conversation was one of the most patronizing I have ever endured. As a matter of social policy, I do not voluntarily convey my formal scientific or educational background in conversations with strangers unless they ask for the information directly. Not knowing my background, he must have thought me to be an ungrateful moron to question his popcorn tutorial.

My father-in-law is an MIT engineer with a scientific pedigree traceable to the post–World War II nuclear arms effort. During the hilltop reception, at a point where his attention was no longer needed by the photographers or by other wedding matters, he walked up to the two of us. I don't know whether my father-in-law had overheard the tone of our banter and felt that I needed to be rescued, but his first comment to me was, "Neil, do you still teach astrophysics at Princeton University?"

This simple eight-word question conveyed eye-popping data to my patronizing partner that cut through his intellectual aggression. His tone instantly became humble and docile, and he even started to ask scientific questions of me, but he never explicitly apologized for his behavior. We ended up friends by the end of the reception, with him asking about the latest theories on big bang cosmology and on the search for other planets in the galaxy.

I actually find it amusing when people who do not know me, and who I have never met, assume me to be deeply ignorant. Sometimes their behavior persists even when I make comments that clearly require years of academic study or other intellectual investment. I once walked into a posh wine shop on the Upper West Side of Manhattan in New York City and noticed a bottle of red Bordeaux on the shelf from a particular château and from a particular vintage that I had been in search of for some time. The bottle was seventeen years old, which is not a particularly unusual specimen for a fine wine shop. As I reached for the bottle to inspect it, the wine merchant, who I later learned was also the owner, barked from across the store, "Don't touch the bottle, it's very old and expensive." I replied, "How else am I to decide whether to buy it?" At which point he grudgingly allowed me to lift it off the rack. I then looked through the glass of the wine bottle, toward an incandescent lamp, to judge the wine's color. If it had been stored poorly over the years, the wine's deep, brilliant garnet color would have prematurely turned amber and then brown. After I told him that the wine was turning sooner than a Bordeaux of that age and vintage should, he suggested that it was the dust on the bottle that was brown rather than the wine itself.

How many more hints could I give him that I knew what I was talking about? After a few more minutes of this charade I politely left the store, went home, and wrote him a letter that I sent via overnight FedEx delivery. After reminding him of our encounter the previous day, my otherwise cordial letter included the following comments:

> *You must have assumed me to be a fool and your-*
> *self to be a wine expert, but clearly the relevant*
> *facts suggest just the opposite. Your actions yester-*
> *day . . . [discredited] yourself as an honest wine*
> *merchant. Perhaps your other clientele won't know*
> *the difference, but if I were you, I would be a little*
> *more careful about what you assume to be the*
> *background of your customers.*

I went on to tell him:

> *If you cannot rise above your prejudice, then I sim-*
> *ply ask to be treated with respect—not because of*
> *my extensive wine knowledge, but simply because I*
> *was a customer who was prepared to spend money*
> *in your store.*

If I were a different character, I could make a lot of money based on this inherent social discrepancy, as others have already done. Depending on the time of year and on the time of day, you can find rows of chess tables near major New York City tourist centers such as Times Square, or near heavily visited public spaces such as Battery Park or Union Square. For $20 or $40 in cash you can place a bet that you will beat the seated person in a game of speed chess. Nearly everyone who waits to be challenged is Black or otherwise quite urban in dress and manner. The passersby are typically White tourists or businessmen who see this as an opportunity to win some fast cash during their lunch break. They might have been star chess players in their high school or college days, or perhaps they just like the game and can't imagine being beaten by a Black person at something that requires intelligence and nimble thinking. After all, you are not betting that you will beat him in a slam-dunk basketball contest. In either case, a flippant assumption gets made about the relative cognitive capacity of the passerby and the chess-player-in-waiting.

In every case that I have witnessed, the White person lost the game.

In another scenario, I had been trying on shoes in a central New Jersey mall. When nothing suited my tastes I left the store empty-handed, except for my shopping bag filled with purchases from other stores in the mall. As I passed those metal security loops at the exit door the alarms went off. The security guard stopped me in my tracks and (politely) asked to look in my shopping bag. Meanwhile, the actual shoplifter, a White woman who passed the security loops at the exact moment that I had, walked free and clear from the store.

What a brilliant shoplifting scheme! Complete with the poetic justice of a store suffering directly from its own prejudice.

Where and when are all these assumptions born? Do people really think that all Blacks are crime-ridden and inherently less intelligent (or just stupid) and that whatever status they achieve is the product of affirmative action and of opportunities that they do not deserve? Occasionally, one sees court cases of White students denied admission to one institution or another because minorities gained special access to 10 percent of the slots. One could just as easily interpret these same cases as White people who failed to be selected for 90 percent of the slots because their record was so poor.

I don't suppose I will ever know how far I have gotten in life through the formal or informal application of affirmative action policies. My grades were certainly all over the place throughout my years in school, almost regardless of the course's level of difficulty. As noted earlier, however, they included the highest GPA in the entire seventh grade of a junior high school in Lexington, Massachusetts, a well-to-do suburb of Boston. My grades also include the highest score in the Bronx High School of Science on the junior year math Regents exam, and the 99th percentile on the mathematics SAT. And in my adult life I have authored five books. Do I deserve special treatment for the color of my skin? I don't know. But what I do know is that in spite of people assuming that I am intellectually incapable, I have retained enough confidence in myself to treat these encounters as the entertaining sideshows that they are.

I am certain, however, that many others do not share my same thickness of skin to withstand this constant onslaught on one's intelligence and ambitions. I occasionally wonder how I have survived it myself.

# FOUR

# ROMANCING THE COSMOS

## FOR THE LOVE OF THE UNIVERSE

I ULTIMATELY DID REACH THE MOUNTAINTOP—that coveted destination I had sought ever since my first view of the night sky though binoculars back in elementary school. Actually I reached many mountains, beginning with the McDonald Observatory of the University of Texas, located on Mount Locke in West Texas, one of the most remote (and darkest) regions within the continental United States. My first research paper, published while in graduate school, was based on data I obtained with a collaborator at the McDonald Observatory.

Other mountain hideaways include the Hale Observatories of Mount Palomar, Southern California, and the Kitt Peak National Observatories of Kitt Peak, Arizona. These telescopes happen to be relatively easy to reach. Other sites require extensive travel arrangements. One such trip is to the Cerro

Tololo Inter-American Observatory (CTIO) in the Andes Mountains of Chile, where I have conducted more research on the universe than at any other telescope in the world.

Although I am a city slicker to the bone, I must confess that mountains are special places. Some of my deepest thoughts and inspiration for life have come to me while on a mountain. The clarity of the air somehow translates into clarity of thought. I suppose I'm not alone here. Mountains have a rich history for inspiring thought and action. What else would drive otherwise rational people to climb mountains for no other reason than just to see what's on the other side. Furthermore, Moses received the Ten Commandments on a mountain, not in a valley. Mohammed was happy to move to the mountain if the mountain would not move to him. Noah parked his ark on a mountain after the waters abated. And in Martin Luther King Jr.'s prophetic speech, delivered on April 3, 1968, the day before he was assassinated, he proclaimed, "I've been to the mountaintop . . . And I've seen the Promised Land. I may not get there with you. But I want you to know that we as a people will get to the Promised Land."

I conceived my Ph.D. convocation speech, the most important of my life, on a mountain. And if the roof of my Skyview apartment building classifies as a mountaintop, then a lot of inspirational stuff happened there too. But the Cerro Tololo Inter-American Observatory in Chile remains closest to my scientific soul.

The nighttime sky from CTIO in Earth's Southern Hemisphere offers a different assortment and orientation of cosmic objects from the North. In particular, at thirty degrees south latitude—the location of CTIO—the center of the Milky Way galaxy rises at sunset, sets at sunrise, and passes directly over-head at midnight in June. A large part of my research interests focus on the structure of our Milky Way within about three de-grees of the galactic center, otherwise known as the galactic bulge, which is a slightly flattened spherical region packed with over 10 billion stars—about 10 percent of the galaxy's total. When observing the nearest galaxies, one can typically identify only the brightest of its giant stars. The remaining bil-lions blur into puddles of light. For this reason, the ability to observe individual stars in our own galaxy provides a unique platform to understand the structure and formation of all spiral galaxies.

To meet the galactic bulge, one must first submit, half a year in advance, an observing proposal that outlines an idea, de-fends its worthiness as a scientific project, and describes in de-tail the requisite hardware needed to achieve the objectives. Observing time is awarded competitively, where the oversub-scription rate can approach a factor of five for the largest of a mountain's array of telescopes. Telescope allocation commit-tees parcel out time in blocks as short as two nights but are typically four to six nights. In the time allocation, no allowance is made for bad weather where bad weather can simply mean overcast skies.

A week or two before the observing run, I prepare detailed coordinates, assemble finding charts, and collect the assorted manuals and notes from previous observing runs that might serve my needs at the telescope. Then comes the trip. When you're flying the five thousand miles due south from the New York metropolitan area to Santiago in June, the local time does not change, which is positively no help when your ultimate mission is to be awake at night and asleep during the day. You will never find an astrophysicist who complains about ordinary jet lag, because the largest possible jet lag is twelve hours, and this is precisely what you get when you invert your schedule to become nocturnal. In this effort, a time zone change would only assist the shift in schedule.

The typical pilgrimage requires a two-and-a-half hour flight to the Miami International Airport, a two-hour layover, a seven-and-a-half hour flight to the Santiago International Airport, a forty-minute (hazardous) taxi ride to the CTIO "Guest House" in downtown Santiago, an eight-hour layover, a twenty-minute (less hazardous) taxi ride to the Santiago bus station, a seven-hour bus ride north—up the coast along the Andes Mountains—to the La Serena administrative headquarters of CTIO, a night at headquarters, and then a one-and-a-half-hour van ride up the Elquí Valley to the summit of Cerro Tololo. The warm clothes I have brought insulate me from the cold of the Chilean mountain winter. I also maintain a keen eye to the sky for the giant South American condors, whose effortless ascent on the mountain thermals portends a night of difficult observing. Once on the mountaintop, I have twenty-four hours to complete the nocturnal inversion before my date with the photons of light from the galactic bulge begins.

Or one can look at it another way. The well-traveled photons began their journey near the center of our galaxy about twenty-six thousand years ago, which renders them contemporaries of Cro-Magnon. My journey, much shorter perhaps, but with no less drama, began three days before. We meet at a detector in the focal plane of the telescope.

I can't help contemplating the fate of those photons not collected by the telescope's giant mirror. Imagine a journey of twenty-six thousand light years only to miss the telescope and slam into the mountainside. Most photons, however, miss Earth completely and are still in motion through interstellar space. But those I collect—those snatched from the photon stream—are what provide the basis for cosmic discovery in my research career.

The moment has arrived. Time is cherished. Clouds are despised. Photons are coveted. The observatory is now my temple—complete with a dome, a telescope, and the dimly lighted control room with its two dozen computer monitors that stream continuously updated information about the telescope, the detector, the object being observed, the ongoing data reductions, and the local weather.

Assisting me in the control room, on one particular trip, is a renowned colleague and friend of mine who is a pure theorist, which simply means he does not necessarily know one end of a telescope from the other. We are two out of three collaborators on a project to obtain original data on the abundance of heavy elements and the velocities through space for thousands of stars. We will use these data to decode some details of the history and structure of the galactic bulge. My theorist colleague had never been to a large optical telescope, so I thought it would be a good idea to haul him all the way to Cerro Tololo. But five hours after he enters the observatory building, central Chile experiences a 6.5 earthquake; the detector's optics are shaken out of alignment and several hours of data are corrupted. Either the observer gods were upset because a pure theorist entered sacred ground, or the Andes Mountains are geologically active. Regardless, next time I may leave him at home.

Back at Princeton University, the department offices are equipped with powerful computer workstations where we conduct extensive data reduction and analysis. In a manner not unlike the methods by which paleontologists interpret time scales from fossil evidence in sedimentary rock, we infer a history of star formation from the enrichment of heavy elements among its stars. As prescribed by the big bang, the first gas clouds—and the first generation of stars formed from them—were composed of pure hydrogen and helium. Most of the elements heavier than these two in the universe owe their origin to supernovae, titanic explosions of high-mass stars in their death throes. Loaded with heavy elements, ejected matter from supernovae mixed with the gas clouds from which the next generation of stars formed. For each subsequent generation of stars, the total enrichment of heavy elements rises.

While some stars die shortly after they are born, most live for many billions of years so that when we observe the galactic bulge we see a beehive mixture of eons of stellar generations. The number of stars that have few heavy elements when compared with the number that have many heavy elements can help to untangle the history of star formation. And by tagging each star with a velocity in space and a location in the galaxy, we derive useful information about the mass, the gravity, and the origin of the bulge's structure.

To draw scientific conclusions of high confidence requires data of high quality. An excellent night at the telescope requires the very best atmospheric conditions. From the uneven heating and cooling of Earth's surface, however, the lower atmosphere can be a turbulent place of rising and falling air currents. What was good for ascending condors on mountain thermals is bad for astrophysicists. One consequence is that a star's image becomes an undulating blob of light on the detector, which seriously compromises observing efficiency and data quality. For your own safety, do not ever tell an astrophysicist, "I hope all your stars are twinkling."

As you climb through the lower atmosphere the pressure drops exponentially, so that the top of a mere 7,000-foot mountain—the altitude of Cerro Tololo Observatory—sits higher than nearly 25 percent of Earth's air molecules, with a corresponding 25 percent drop in atmospheric pressure. These observing conditions dramatically improve most astronomical data. A mountain twice this height, such as Mauna Kea in Hawaii (home of many of the world's largest optical telescopes), rises above 40 percent of Earth's atmosphere and is the location of some of the finest ground-based observations ever made.

That mountains tend to be ideal venues for cosmic inquiry did not escape Sir Isaac Newton in his 1704 treatise on optics. He hypothesized:

> *If the Theory of making Telescopes could at length be fully brought into Practice, yet there would be certain Bounds beyond which Telescopes could not perform. For the Air through which we look upon the Stars, is in a perpetual Tremor; as may be seen by the . . . twinkling of the fix'd Stars.*

Sir Isaac continued with telescopic foresight:

> *The only Remedy is a most serene and quiet Air, such as may perhaps be found on the tops of the highest Mountains above the Grosser Clouds.*

An even better "Remedy" is found in the well-publicized Hubble Space Telescope, which was lifted into orbit primarily to escape the degraded image quality and poor resolution that the lower atmosphere imposes on observations of all objects.

The thin air has its drawbacks, however. While living nocturnally during the long Chilean winter nights, I must sustain a level of alertness and intellectual intensity that is without counterpart in everyday life. On the mountain, each breath draws one-fourth less oxygen than at sea level, yet I am in computer command of millions of dollars' worth of high-precision optics and hardware. The stress forces me to reach a self-induced state of cosmic stimulation. Only while observing do I reflect on how many times in a normal day my mind drifts away from peak intensity through built-in mental pauses such as coffee breaks, lunch breaks, mail breaks, and the occasional stare out of my office window.

I end the final night of the observing sessions as I listen to one of those bombastic classical music finales on the observatory dome's CD player. Often the twenty-odd thumps that end the fourth movement of Beethoven's Ninth Symphony do just fine. I close the observatory slit, which generates a sound that, as you might suspect, resonates in the telescope dome with the acoustic richness of a cathedral. Dark time, that most coveted sequence of observing nights where the Moon is near its new phase, ensures that at the end of an observing run of more than four or five days, morning twilight will contain the rising thin crescent moon low on the horizon, framed in the layered colors of the dawn sky. When viewed from a mountaintop, the pre-sunrise horizon light is no less bright than when viewed from sea level, but the surrounding sky that has yet to be absorbed by dawn is much deeper in its darkness. The result is a stirring sweep from the rich remains of the night sky overhead to the radiant twilight on the eastern horizon.

With my little piece of the universe written to a high capacity data tape in my breast pocket, I now return home with two backup tapes secured—one in my checked luggage, and one left behind on the mountain.

But times change.

Through my joint appointment at Princeton University's Department of Astrophysical Sciences, we are part of a consortium of a half-dozen institutions that own and operate a 3.5 meter telescope at Apache Point, New Mexico. Apache Point is the 9,200-foot summit of a cliff face near Sunspot, New Mexico, home of the National Solar Observatory, which is around the corner from the mountain resort town of Cloudcroft, New Mexico. What makes the Apache Point telescope unusual is that it was conceived and constructed to be run remotely over internet lines from independent control rooms located at each member site. The Princeton control room was carved into a specially outfitted space in the department's basement. In principle, the only difference between observing remotely at Apache Point and observing on location at Cerro Tololo is the "length of the wires" that connect to the back of each computer console.

For many types of observing projects, now all I need do is walk for about ninety seconds from my office door to the basement observing room. Yes, it looks and smells and feels like a real observing room—complete with a CD player, a coffee machine, and subdued lighting. But as efficient as remote observing is, one cannot deny the absence of a mountain's majesty. For better or for worse, I suppose there will come a time when

I tell my grand-graduate students: "Back in the old days, the data didn't just appear on our doorsteps. We traveled great distances. We ascended great mountains. We met the universe and its photons face-to-face."

The history of discovery in the physical sciences forms a continuous braid, woven of theoretical and experimental triumphs. Occasionally, a scientist is talented at both, but one's formal training is usually either as a theorist or an experimentalist. In the astrophysical sciences, where laboratory tests of cosmic phenomena are few, experimentalists are more accurately described as observers who, more than likely, use mountaintop telescopes.

Observers and theoreticians are fundamentally different. If an observer's data have a history of being flawed (through inferior methodology or because nobody can reproduce the observation), then future data published by that person may be regarded as suspect—especially if the data overthrow well-tested ideas or hint at brand-new phenomena. Conversely, when armed with pencil and paper and some equations, the theorist can be wrong many times, as long as an interesting path is taken. Interesting paths often contain keys to further discovery.

In pure math, an algebraic equation simply needs to have its left side numerically equal its right side, and the equation need not relate in any way to the real world. In the physical universe, however, equations connect measured quantities such as temperatures, energy, velocities, and forces. Someone locked away in a closet can therefore deduce all manner of mathematical theorems (if so inclined) but would unlikely walk out as a leading theoretical physicist. Nature has unlimited power of veto on the ideas of physicists, while mathematicians are accountable only to math's self-contained logic. Behold the primary reason why child prodigies exist among mathematicians but not among physicists.

The mathematics of cosmic discovery contains a language of complicated-looking algebraic equations. Some are beautiful, others are ugly, but they all are nothing more than the mathematical representation of a physical idea. What distinguishes theories rooted in equations from theories rooted in armchair speculation is that the mathematical image of your ideas forces those ideas—and the deductions drawn from them—to be logically constructed. Arguably the most amazing thing about mathematics, which is a pure invention of the human mind, is that it actually works as a tool to help us decode the universe. There was no tablet in the sky that declared the universe to be mathematically describable. We just figured out that it was. Without math, science would not exist as we know it today.

When I first took calculus in eleventh grade at the Bronx High School of Science, I remember seeing columns and columns of esoteric equations that filled the front and rear inside flaps of the course's textbook. Though elegant, the notation was entirely unfamiliar. The meaning and purpose of the symbols were unknown to me. Half the school year would pass before the fog lifted and I learned all about them. They included derivatives and integrals—elegant ways that calculus operates on changing quantities in nature. The calculus I was learning was what Sir Isaac Newton invented to describe why planets orbited the Sun in the shape of ellipses. I felt enlightened, empowered, and energized to learn more and more math so that no part of the physical universe would be out of my reach.

I am convinced that the act of thinking logically cannot possibly be natural to the human mind. If it were, then mathematics would be everybody's easiest course in school and our species would not have taken several millennia to figure out the scientific method. If you fear equations, then you are not alone. In the preface of the best-selling book *A Brief History of Time*, Stephen Hawking reflects on a comment from a publisher friend that for every equation he chose to include, the number of potential buyers would drop by half. If Hawking included only ten equations in his book, the publisher expected the readership to drop by a factor of one-half raised to the tenth power, leaving just 1/1000 of the potential readers. *A Brief History of Time* was not published equationless, but it contained many fewer than it could have. As we all know, Hawking wrote what came to be one of the biggest-selling science books of all time.

If the sight of equations upsets you, consider that they are generally no more complicated than anything else you might not understand on first sight. For example, the following equation—known as a Maxwellian distribution of speeds, and named for the famous English physicist James Clerk Maxwell (1831–1879)—contains a healthy assortment of symbols:

$$F(v) \, dv = 4\pi n \left(\frac{m}{2\pi \, kT}\right)^{3/2} v^2 \exp\left(-mv^2/2kT\right) dv$$

Like many important equations that describe the universe, it is a distribution function, which is a slightly more sophisticated version of the bar charts that are common in daily newspapers that are prone to pictographs such as *USA Today*. These types of equations tell us how various features of the universe are organized. For a given temperature the Maxwellian distribution of velocities enables us to calculate the fraction of all gas molecules that happen to be moving within a designated range of speed.

When applied to the molecular activity within Earth's lower atmosphere, you can use it to calculate the speed with which the largest number of air molecules moves. It's about 450 meters per second. From this speed you can further calculate (using another formula, of course) the speed of sound through air, which is a closely related quantity.

As I acquired knowledge of math and physics through high school, college, and graduate school, the workings of the world around me became more and more transparent. I could understand, describe, and predict phenomena that previously fell out of my reach and out of my grasp.

Learning what the above equations do required fifteen seconds of time to read each paragraph that encloses them. Appreciating the full depth and soul of the equations so that you can use them to communicate with others requires extensive study. But the equations of physics are no more cryptic than communication channels found in other disciplines. For instance, nearly everybody knows that deoxyribonucleic acid is DNA, the molecule that encodes the identity of all known forms of life, but years of study would only begin to achieve a full understanding of its function. Or take *Pachycephalosaurus*, which any eight-year-old child knows is a funny-looking dinosaur with a bulbous, knobby head. But understanding its designation as a genus requires some training far beyond the simple memorization of its name. Biology and chemistry are infamous for their cryptic names of things. One of my favorites is oxymetazoline hydrochloride, which happens to be the active ingredient in my twelve-hour nasal spray. It clears my stuffy nose. But beyond that, I'll need to take a course in pharmacology to understand how and why it works in my nasal passages. And the following four lines from the Prologue to Chaucer's *Canterbury Tales*, penned in Middle English, require no small amount of homework to decode and understand:

> *And smale foweles maken melodye*
> *That slepen al the nyght with open yë*
> *(So priketh hem nature in hir corages);*
> *Thanne longen folk to goon on pilgrimages.*

So don't complain about the obscurity of my equations. Besides, unlike other forms of cryptic communication, equations enable us to predict with high precision the nature and behavior of cosmic phenomena. The long history of religious cults that form around those who claim special powers to predict the future alerts us to the fact that your average scientist could create the most devoted cult the world has ever seen. All a scientist needs to do is hide the equations and the methods from view and reveal to the followers only the predictions: "The Sun will rise tomorrow at 7:02 A.M." "A comet with two dozen large pieces will slam into Jupiter's atmosphere." "The midday Sun will be eaten by darkness." The subject would make a good sociology novel.

Some of an equation's obscurity can, of course, be blamed

on the presence of unfamiliar symbols. These days, it's hard to find an equation that does not use one or more squiggly letters from a foreign alphabet. And the alphabets don't come squigglier than lower-case Greek. In sequence from alpha to omega we have: α β γ δ ε ζ η θ ι κ λ μ ν ξ ο π ρ σ τ υ Φ χ ψ ω. The most famous among them is probably the letter pi: π. Pi normally represents the exact ratio of a circle's circumference to its diameter, and thus makes cameo appearances in all manner of equations that contain references to geometry—from the area of a circle to the shape of the universe. By the way, you can always remember the formula for the area of a circle because, as the saying goes, pi are not round, pi are squared. In other "words," $A = \pi r^2$. At least half of the lower-case Greek letters are in regular use by astrophysicists and represent selected physical quantities.

We also tap the upper-case letters of the Greek alphabet: A B Γ Δ E Z H Θ I K Λ M N Ξ O Π P Σ T Y Φ X Ψ Ω, although many resemble letters from our familiar Roman alphabet. In cosmology, the study of the origin and fate of the universe, the most widely used symbol is omega: Ω. Defined as the ratio of the actual density of mass in the universe to a "critical" density, its value tells us whether or not our expanding universe will one day recollapse due to the collective gravity of all cosmic matter. Using the lower-case Greek letter rho ($\rho$) to represent density, the relation reads:

$$\Omega = \rho / \rho_{crit} .$$

Equations are not ideas unto themselves. They are just the symbols that represent ideas. This subtle but important distinction enables quadriplegic Stephen Hawking to deduce the nature of the universe in his head, without having to write the equations on a piece of paper.

As serious as equations can be, their world is not entirely humorless. If an equation happens to have too many Greek letters, you have my permission to say, "It's Greek to me." And if you are mathematically disinclined, yet you nonetheless want to make a splash at a party of engineers or physicists, I promise that the following riddle is sure to make them all bust open with laughter:

Q: *What do you get when you cross a rabbit with an elephant?*
A: *Rabbit elephant sine theta.*

The above riddle is hilarious because there is a mathematical operation called a "cross product," which takes two quantities, each having a magnitude and a direction (such as two velocities or two forces), and multiplies their magnitudes with the sine of theta ($\theta$)——the angle between the directions they point. The sine function is one of those operations in trigonometry that you were certain you would never see again after high school. Mathematically, the cross product reads

$$| \, A \times B \, | = A \, B \, sine \, \theta$$

where the flanking $|\ |$ symbols provide instructions to calculate the magnitude of the result. In an admittedly absurd algebraic substitution, you set $A$ = *rabbit* and $B$ = *elephant* and you recover the structure of the original riddle. No later than the first year in college, every physics and engineering student learns about cross products and other valuable ways to combine physical quantities.

I first saw the following relation on a bathroom wall in my high school.

$$\int e^x = f(\mathrm{u})^n$$

The long and skinny S-shaped symbol was developed by the famous seventeenth-century German mathematician Gottfreid Leibniz as a stylized letter *S* representing a sum. While not constructed to be a bona fide equation, it does beg to be read as *sex = fun*. Such was the "filthy" bathroom humor of my high school.

My vote for the most profound equations ever conceived goes to a set that, as before, bear the name of the English physicist James Clerk Maxwell. Containing a complete description of the behavior and propagation of electromagnetic waves (i.e. light), Maxwell's equations occupy the summit of classical (pre-twentieth-century) physics. I reproduce them below not because I expect you to calculate with them but because they are beautiful and they reveal a remarkable asymmetry in the universe.

$$\nabla \cdot \mathbf{E} = 4 \pi \rho$$
$$\nabla \times \mathbf{E} = -\frac{1}{c} \frac{\partial \mathbf{B}}{\partial t}$$
$$\nabla \cdot \mathbf{B} = 0$$
$$\nabla \times \mathbf{B} = \frac{1}{c} \frac{\partial \mathbf{E}}{\partial t} + \frac{4\pi}{c} \mathbf{J}$$

The **E** stands for electric field, the **B** stands for magnetic field, and the **J** stands for a current of moving charges. In what was formerly considered to be two separate notions, both electricity and magnetism were conjoined in Maxwell's equations to represent a single physical entity known as electromagnetism. Notice also the upside-down pyramid (a special operator) accompanied by a dot next to the letter **E** in the first line. This particular equation describes the behavior of an electric field around charged objects. The counterpart equation for magnetic fields appears on the third line. But the equation equals zero. By a little-understood fluke of nature, the universe contains isolatable electrical charges (pluses and minuses) but no isolatable magnetic charges. What this means is that north poles of magnets always come attached to south poles. Try it. Go home and smash a magnet into smithereens. Each piece will spontaneously become a N–S magnet, no matter how small or large the fragments are. In physics vernacular, the universe contains no monopoles (as revealed in Maxwell's equations), which remains one of the great mysteries of the cosmos.

If you want to know more about Maxwell's equations, they require a background in vector calculus and electrodynamics, which I will not introduce at this time.

Some equations are symmetric and relatively simple, depending on the coordinate system in which they are constructed. Expressed in familiar $x$, $y$, and $z$ coordinates, a widely used equation to probe the spatial shape of many things (including the force of gravity), is called the Laplacian operator, named for the brilliant French mathematician Pierre-Simon de Laplace (1749–1827):

$$\nabla^2 = \frac{\partial^2}{\partial x^2} + \frac{\partial^2}{\partial y^2} + \frac{\partial^2}{\partial z^2}$$

As a smooth operator, the equation acts as though it were a machine in an assembly line. You feed it a mathematical function and out comes a representation of that function's behavior in three-dimensional space. In many cases, the Laplacian operator is easier to use when you transform $x$, $y$, and $z$ into the spherical coordinates of $r$, $\theta$, and $\phi$, which is the natural coordinate system for spherical objects such a stars and galaxy halos. But it now takes on an intimidating air that has made strong men weep:

$$\nabla^2 = \frac{1}{r^2} \frac{\partial}{\partial r}\left(r^2\frac{\partial}{\partial r}\right) + \frac{1}{r^2\sin\theta} \frac{\partial}{\partial \theta}\left(\sin\theta\frac{\partial}{\partial \theta}\right) + \frac{1}{r^2\sin^2\theta} \frac{\partial^2}{\partial \phi^2}$$

At the Bronx High School of Science, the number of mathematical functions on your pocket calculator earned you more popularity credits than whether you were a star athlete. Immediately after learning of Maxwell's equations, one classmate of mine named Franck Larece fantasized about a set of mathematical relations that would one day be known as the "Larece Equations." Since I had already learned about Laplace and his equally brilliant contemporary Joseph-Louis Lagrange (1736–1813), for me it was not a stretch to imagine the name "Larece" among them.

If your name becomes associated with fertile equations then you become forever linked to continuing pathways of discovery. For example, after some additional mathematical tools were developed by Laplace, Newton's equations of gravity could be adapted to infer the existence of a theretofore undiscovered planet in the outer solar system. Its gravity had been tugged on the orbit of Uranus, forcing it to move in ways that seemed to violate Newton's laws. Sure enough, the planet Neptune was discovered just about where it was predicted to be.

Mercury's orbit also happens to behave in ways that seem to violate the predictions of Newton's laws. Mercury's closest approach to the Sun in its oval orbit predictably shifts over time, through the combined tugs of all other sources of gravity in the solar system. However, the observed shift was more than could be credited to Newton's laws once all known sources of gravity, such as the rest of the planets, were reconciled. After the triumphant discovery of Neptune, astronomers were armed and ready. The fellow who predicted the existence and location of Neptune in 1846, Urbain-Jean-Joseph Leverrier (1811-1877), took on the task. Wasting no time, Leverrier proposed, in 1846, a brand-new planet, Vulcan. Named for the Roman god of fire, Vulcan would orbit close to the Sun, providing a gravitational tug on Mercury with just enough force to account for the deviations from Newton's laws. Never mind the fact that such a planet could have (and would have) been detected during the countless total solar eclipses throughout recorded history, Vulcan lived in and among Newton's equations of gravity for seventy years.

When Einstein published the general theory of relativity (the modern theory of gravity) in 1916, his equations showed that in the vicinity of strong sources of gravity Newton's laws do not provide an accurate description of the behavior of matter. The disturbed fabric of space and time alters what one would expect from Newton's laws alone. Sure enough, the deviation in Mercury's closest approach to the Sun was fully accounted for within Einstein's new theories. In the first case, unexplained planetary perturbations led to the prediction and discovery of a new planet. In the second case, unexplained planetary perturbations led to new laws of physics. Such are the schizophrenic paths that lie before the research scientist.

In the history of the physical sciences, when successful theories are supplanted by ones that are more complete, the previous theories (and their attendant equations) don't all of a sudden become ineffective. The genetic links are in place; Einstein's equations look exactly like Newton's equations when you plug in slow speeds and weak gravity. And Newton's equations can be stripped down to look exactly like Johannes Kepler's descriptive laws of planetary motion.

When I solve the unknown quantities within an equation using pencil and paper, I achieve the same level of noble solitude as when I write a letter with a quill pen by candlelight. I become absorbed by the task, which, for complex equations, can last many hours. While en route to the mathematical solution, I forsake food, personal hygiene, and the measurement of time. I have found that when calculating what no one has calculated before, like my observing sessions on the mountain, my mental acuity peaks. Ironically, these are the times that I would flunk the reality check normally reserved for mental patients and dazed boxers: What is your name? What day is it? Who is the President of the United States? During intense computational moments, I do not remember, I do not know, and I do not care. I am at peace with my equations as I connect to the cosmic engines that drive our universe.

# FIVE

# THE END OF THE WORLD

## THE SCIENCE OF CATASTROPHE

FOR SOME PEOPLE, METEORITES ARE TROPHIES to be cherished and displayed. For me, they are harbingers of doom and disaster. Consider that the slowest speed at which a large asteroid can impact Earth is about six or seven miles per second. Imagine getting hit by my overpriced objet d'art moving that fast. You would be squashed like a bug. Imagine one the size of a beach ball. It would obliterate a four-bedroom home. Imagine one a few miles across. It would alter Earth's ecosystem and render extinct the majority of Earth's land species. That's what meteorites mean to me, and it's what they should mean to you because the chances that both of our tombstones will read "killed by asteroid" are about the same as for "killed in an airplane crash."

Amazing but true.

About two dozen people have been killed by falling aster-oids in the past four hundred years, but thousands have died in crashes during the relatively brief history of passenger air travel. The impact record shows that by the end of ten million years, when the sum of all airplane crashes has killed a billion people (assuming a conservative death-by-airplane rate of one hundred per year), an asteroid is likely to have hit Earth with enough energy to kill a billion people. While airplanes kill peo-ple a few at a time, our asteroid might not kill anybody for mil-lions of years. But when it hits, it will take out hundreds of millions of people instantaneously and many more hundreds of millions in the wake of global climatic upheaval.

The combined asteroid and comet impact rate in the early solar system was frighteningly high. Theories of planet forma-tion show that chemically rich gas condenses to form mole-cules, then particles of dust, then rocks and ice. Thereafter, it's a shooting gallery. Collisions serve as a means for chemical and gravitational forces to bind smaller objects into larger ones. Those objects that, by chance, accreted slightly more mass than average will have slightly higher gravity and attract other ob-jects even more. As accretion continues, gravity eventually shapes blobs into spheres and planets are born. The most mas-sive planets had sufficient gravity to retain gaseous envelopes.

All planets continue to accrete for the rest of their days, al-though at a significantly lower rate than when formed. Still, there remain billions (possibly trillions) of comets in the ex-treme outer solar system, orbiting up to a thousand times the size of Pluto's orbit. They all are susceptible to gravitational nudges from passing stars and interstellar clouds that set them on their long journey inward toward the Sun. Solar system leftovers also include short-period comets, of which two dozen are known to cross Earth's orbit, and thousands of catalogued asteroids, of which at least one hundred do the same.

On the return trip across the country from my summer at Camp Uraniborg, we took a detour to visit Meteor Crater in Arizona. The juxtaposition of appearance with accurate knowledge can be the most humbling force on the human soul. On first sight, the crater is simply an enormous hole in the ground—fourteen football fields across and deep enough to bury a sixty-story building. With the Grand Canyon a few hundred miles away, Arizona is no stranger to holes in the ground. But to carve the Grand Canyon, Mother Earth required millions of years. To excavate Meteor Crater, Mother Universe, using a sixty-thousand-ton asteroid traveling upward of twenty miles per second, required a tenth of a second. No offense to Grand Canyon lovers, but for my money, Meteor Crater is the most amazing natural landmark in the world.

The polite (and scientifically accurate) word for asteroid impacts is "accretion." I happen to prefer "species-killing, ecosystem-destroying event." But from the point of view of solar system history, the terms are the same. We cannot simultaneously be happy we live on a planet; happy that our planet is chemically rich; and happy we are not dinosaurs; yet resent the risk of planetwide catastrophe.

Some of the energy of an asteroid collision with Earth gets deposited into our atmosphere through friction and an airburst of shock waves. Sonic booms are shock waves too, but airplanes typically make them by traveling at speeds anywhere between one and three times the speed of sound. The worst damage an ordinary sonic boom might do is jiggle the dishes in your cabinet. But with speeds upward of forty-five thousand miles per hour—nearly seventy times the speed of sound—the shock waves from your average collision between an asteroid and Earth can be devastating.

If the asteroid (or comet) is large enough to survive its own shock waves, the rest of its energy is deposited on Earth in an explosive event that heats the ground and blows a crater that can measure twenty times the diameter of the original object. If many impactors strike with little time between each event, then Earth's surface will not have enough time to cool between impacts. We infer from the pristine cratering record on the surface of the Moon (our nearest neighbor in space) that Earth experienced an era of heavy bombardment between 4.6 billion and 4 billion years ago, when the Earth's surface was unrelentingly sterilized. The formation of complex molecules, and thus life, was inhibited, although all the basic ingredients were being delivered nonetheless. The oldest fossil evidence for life on Earth dates from about 3.8 billion years ago. An often-quoted figure for life to emerge is 800 million years (4.6 billion - 3.8 billion = 800 million). But to be fair to organic chemistry, you must first subtract all the time Earth's surface was forbiddingly hot. That leaves a mere 200 million years over which life emerged from a rich chemical soup, which, as do all good soups, includes water.

Yes, much of the water you drink each day was delivered to Earth by comets more than four billion years ago. But not all space debris are leftovers from the beginning of the solar system. Earth has been hit at least a dozen times by rocks ejected from Mars, and we've been hit countless more times by rocks ejected from the Moon. Ejection occurs when impactors carry so much energy that smaller rocks near the impact zone are thrust upward with sufficient speed to escape the gravitational grip of the planet. Afterward, the rocks mind their own ballistic business in orbit around the Sun until they slam into something. The most famous of the Mars rocks is the first meteorite found near the Alan Hills section of Antarctica in 1984. Officially known by its coded, though sensible abbreviation, ALH84001, this meteorite contains tantalizing though circumstantial evidence that simple life on the Red Planet thrived a billion years ago. As noted earlier, a frenzy of media attention greeted this announcement, made in 1996 by a team led by NASA scientists.

Mars has boundless "geo"logical evidence for a history of running water that includes dried riverbeds, river deltas, and flood plains. Since liquid water is crucial to the survival of life as we know it, the possibility of life on Mars does not stretch scientific credulity. The fun part comes when you speculate whether life arose on Mars first, was blasted off its surface as the solar system's first bacterial astronaut, and then arrived to jump-start Earth's own evolution of life. There's even a word for the process: panspermia. Maybe we are all Martians.

The claims for life on ALH84001 remain controversial, as are most claims on the frontier of cosmic discovery. All the more reason to get up and go to Mars to collect more data. In the meantime, matter is far more likely to travel all by itself from Mars to Earth than vice versa. Escaping Earth's gravity requires over two and a half times the energy than that required to leave Mars. Furthermore, Earth's atmosphere is about one hundred times denser. Air resistance on Earth (relative to Mars) is formidable.

Martian bacteria would have to be hardy indeed to survive the several million years of interplanetary wanderings before landing on Earth. Fortunately, there is no shortage of liquid water and rich chemistry on Earth, so we do not require theories of panspermia to explain the origin of life as we know it, even if we still cannot explain it.

Ironically, we can (and do) blame impacts for major episodes of extinction in the fossil record. Seventy percent of Earth's surface is water and over 99 percent is uninhabited, so you would expect nearly all impactors to hit either the ocean or desolate regions on Earth's surface. So why do movie meteors have such good aim? Especially egregious examples include the 1998 film *Armageddon*, where an incoming meteor decapitates New York City's Chrysler Building, and the 1997 television miniseries *Asteroid*, where a meteor squarely hits a dam in Kansas and floods the nearby town. If you are a movie producer, you can still have a grand time destroying all life on Earth. All you need to do is have the asteroid hit the ocean and have the impact include global tsunamis that wash the world's coastal cities down the drain.

Some famous impact sites in the world include the 1908 explosion near the Tunguska River, Siberia, which felled thousands of square kilometers of trees and incinerated the three hundred square kilometers near ground zero. The impactor was likely a sixty-meter stony meteorite (about the size of a twenty-story building) that exploded in midair, thus leaving no crater. Collisions of this magnitude happen, on average, every couple of centuries. The two-hundred-kilometer diameter Chicxulub Crater in the Yucatán, Mexico, is likely to have been left by a ten-kilometer asteroid. With an impact energy five billion times greater than the atomic bombs exploded in World War II, such a collision might occur about once in million years. The Chicxulub Crater dates from sixty-five million years ago, and there hasn't been one of its magnitude since. Coincidentally, at about the same time, *Tyrannosaurus rex* and friends became extinct, enabling mammals to evolve into something more ambitious than tree shrews.

Those paleontologists and geologists who remain in denial of the role of cosmic impacts in the extinction record of Earth's species must figure out what else to do with the deposit of energy being delivered to Earth from space. Most impactors with less than about ten megatons of energy will explode in the atmosphere and leave no trace of a crater. The few that survive in one piece to leave a crater are likely to be iron-based.

Fortunately, among the population of Earth-crossing asteroids, we have a chance at cataloguing everything larger than about a kilometer—the size that begins to wreak global catastrophe. An early-warning and defense system to protect the human species from these impactors is a realistic goal. Unfortunately, objects smaller than about a kilometer do not reflect enough light to be reliably detected and tracked. These can hit us without notice, or they can hit with notice that is much too short for us do anything about it. The bright side of this news is that while they have enough energy to create local catastrophe by incinerating entire nations, they will not put the human species at risk of extinction. Have a nice day.

The more I study the risk of impacts, the more tentative life on Earth feels to me. Perhaps I know too much to be calm. In the 1998 disaster film *Deep Impact*, a comet does hit the

Atlantic Ocean (instead of a landmark building in a famous city) and punches forth a tidal wave that wipes out the coastal cities of North America, especially New York City. I saw the building in which I currently reside topple like a domino against other buildings in lower Manhattan, as the wall of water plowed through the city and up the Hudson Valley. We, as a species, are utterly helpless in the face of common disasters such as tornadoes, hurricanes, volcanoes, earthquakes, and tsunamis. We can neither control them nor stop them. Yet, the worst of them pale when compared with the devastation a killer asteroid can bring.

Of course, Earth is not the only rocky planet at risk of impacts. Mercury has a cratered face that, to a casual observer, looks just like the Moon. Recent radio topography of cloud-enshrouded Venus shows no shortage of craters either. And Mars, with its historically active geology, reveals large craters that were recently formed.

Earth's fossil record teems with extinct species—life forms that had thrived far longer than the current Earth tenure of *Homo sapiens.* Dinosaurs are on this list. What defense do we have against such formidable impact energies? The battle cry of those with no war to fight is "blow them out of the sky with nuclear weapons." True, the most efficient package of destructive energy ever conceived by humans is nuclear power. A direct hit on an incoming asteroid might explode it into enough small pieces to reduce the impact danger to a harmless, though spectacular, meteor shower. (In empty space, where there is no air, there can be no shock waves, so a nuclear warhead must actually make contact with the asteroid to do damage.)

Another method engages those radiation-intensive neutron bombs (you remember—they were the variety of bombs that killed people but left the buildings standing) in a way that the high-energy neutron bath heats one side of the asteroid to sufficient temperature that material spews forth and the asteroid recoils out of the collision path. A kindler, gentler method is to nudge the asteroid out of harm's way with slow but steady rockets somehow attached to one side. If you do this early enough, then only a small nudge will be required using conventional chemical fuels. If we catalogued every kilometer-size (and larger) object whose orbit intersects Earth's, then a detailed computer calculation would enable us to predict a catastrophic collision hundreds and even thousands of orbits in the future, granting earthlings sufficient time to mount an appropriate defense. But our list of potential killer impactors is woefully incomplete, and our ability to predict the behavior of objects much further into the future (for millions and billions of orbits) is severely compromised by the onset of orbital chaos.

Should we build high-tech missiles that live in silos somewhere awaiting their call to defend the human species? We would first need that detailed inventory of the orbits for all objects that pose a risk to life on Earth. The number of people in the world engaged in this search totals one or two dozen. How long into the future are you willing to protect *Homo sapiens* on Earth? Before you answer that question, take a detour to Arizona's Meteor Crater during your next vacation.

Sometimes it seems that everybody is trying to tell you when and how the "world" is supposed to end. Some scenarios are more familiar than others. Those that are widely discussed in the media include rampant infectious disease, nuclear war, environmental decay, and of course collisions with asteroids or comets. While different in origin, each can induce the end of the human species (and perhaps other selected life forms) on Earth. Implicit in clichéd slogans such as "Save the Earth" is the egocentric call to save life on Earth, not the planet itself.

In fact, humans cannot really save Earth, nor can we really kill Earth. Earth will remain in happy orbit around the Sun, along with its planetary brethren, long after *Homo sapiens* has become extinct by whatever cause. But there are less familiar, though just as real, end-of-world scenarios that jeopardize our temperate planet in its stable orbit around the Sun. I offer these prognostications not because humans are likely to live long enough to observe them, but because the tools of astrophysics enable me to calculate them. Three that come to mind are the death of the Sun, the impending collision between our Milky Way galaxy and the Andromeda galaxy, and the death of the universe, about which the community of astrophysicists has recently achieved consensus.

These scenarios of catastrophe do not worry me on a day-to-day basis because they are slow and steady. But I dream about them and how spectacular they would look if you could speed up time. Computer models of stellar evolution are akin to actuarial tables. They indicate a healthy ten-billion-year life expectancy for our Sun. At an estimated age of five billion years, the Sun has another five billion years of relatively stable energy output. By then, if we have not figured out a way to leave Earth, then we will bear witness to a remarkable evolutionary change in our host star as it runs out of fuel.

The Sun owes its stability to the controlled fusion of hydrogen into helium in its fifteen-million-degree core. The gravity that wants to collapse the star is held in balance by the outward gas pressure that is sustained by the fusion. While more than 90 percent of the Sun's atoms are hydrogen, the ones that matter are those that reside in the core. When the core exhausts its hydrogen, the Sun is left with a central ball of helium atoms that require a higher temperature than does hydrogen to fuse into heavier elements. Now out of balance, gravity wins, the inner regions of the star collapse, and the central temperature rises through one hundred million degrees, which triggers the fusion of helium into carbon.

Along the way, the Sun's luminosity grows astronomically, which forces its outer layers to expand to bulbous proportions, engulfing the orbits of Mercury and Venus. Eventually, the Sun will swell to occupy the entire sky as its expansion nearly subsumes the orbit of Earth. This would be bad. The temperature on Earth will rise until it equals the three-thousand-degree rarefied outer layers of the expanded Sun. Our atmosphere will evaporate away into interplanetary space and the oceans will boil off as Earth becomes a red-hot, charred ember orbiting deep within the Sun. Eventually, the Sun will cease all nuclear fusion, lose its spherical, tenuous, gaseous envelope, and expose its dying central core. Scenarios such as these will one day force manned space travel to become a global priority.

In my first sky show as director of the Hayden Planetarium, I wrote a script called "Cosmic Mind Bogglers." It included a catastrophe or two, just as I had dreamed them to be. For one of the sequences the Sun becomes a red giant as it slowly swells to fill the dome of the sky theater. The event is accompanied by an intensely ominous musical track. It must have worked, because during the month after its premiere, I received dozens of letters from angry parents whose children could not sleep at night for fear of the Sun's fate. The kids must not have paid attention to the part where the show's narrator says, "Five billion years from now . . ."

Not long after the Sun toasts Earth, the Milky Way will encounter some problems of its own. Of the hundreds of thousands of galaxies whose velocity relative to the Milky Way has been measured, only a few are moving toward us while all the rest are moving away at a speed directly related to their distances from us. Discovered in the 1920s by Edwin Hubble (after whom the Hubble Space Telescope was named), the general recession of galaxies is the observational signature of our expanding universe. The Milky Way and the three-hundred-billion-star Andromeda galaxy are close enough to each other that the effect of the expanding universe is negligible. We happen to be drifting toward each other at about one hundred kilometers per second (a quarter million miles per hour). If our (unknown) sideways motion is small, then at this rate, the two-million-light-year distance that separates us will shrink to zero within about seven billion years.

Interstellar space is so vast that there is no need to fear whether stars in the Andromeda galaxy will accidentally slam into the Sun. During the galaxy-galaxy encounter, which would be a spectacular sight from a safe distance, stars are likely to pass each other by. But the event would not be worry-free. Some of Andromeda's stars just may swing close enough to our solar system to influence the orbit of the planets and of the hundreds of billions of resident comets. For example, close stellar flybys can throw one's gravitational allegiance into question. Computer simulations commonly show that the planets are either stolen by the interloper in a "flyby looting" or they become unbound and are flung forth into interplanetary space.

Remember how choosy Goldilocks was with other people's porridge? If we are stolen by the gravity of another star, there is no guarantee that our newfound orbit will be at the right distance to sustain liquid water on Earth's surface—a condition generally agreed to be a prerequisite to sustaining life as we know it. If Earth orbits too close, its water supply evaporates. And if Earth orbits too far, its water supply freezes solid.

By some miracle of future technology, if Earth inhabitants have managed to prolong the life of the Sun, then these efforts will be rendered irrelevant when Earth is flung into space. The absence of a nearby energy source will allow Earth's surface temperature to drop swiftly to hundreds of degrees below zero Fahrenheit. This would also be bad. Our cherished atmosphere of nitrogen and oxygen and other gases would first liquefy and then freeze solid, encrusting the Earth like icing on a cake. We would freeze before we had a chance to starve. The last surviving life on Earth would be those privileged organisms that had evolved to rely not on the Sun's energy but on (what will then be) weak geochemical and geothermal sources, where the heat of Earth's interior emerges from the crust. At the moment, humans are not among them. There will be, of course, other planets that we can visit in orbit around healthy stars in other galaxies.

Even if you manage to stay safe underwater, and evolve to dine upon tasty tube worms at the midocean vents, the long-term fate of the cosmos cannot be postponed or avoided. No matter where you hide, you will be part of a universe that inexorably marches toward a peculiar oblivion. The latest and best evidence available on the space density of matter and the expansion rate of the universe suggests that we are on a one-way trip: The collective gravity of everything in the universe is insufficient to halt and reverse the cosmic expansion.

Currently, the most successful description of the universe and its origin combines the big bang with our modern understanding of gravity, derived from Einstein's general theory of relativity. The early universe was a trillion-degree maelstrom of matter mixed with energy, affectionately known as the primordial soup. During the thirteen-billion-year expansion that followed, the background temperature of the universe has dropped to a mere three degrees on the absolute (Kelvin) temperature scale. As the universe continues to expand, this temperature will continue to approach zero. Such a low background temperature does not directly affect us on Earth because our Sun (normally) grants us a cozy life. But as each generation of stars is born from the interstellar gas clouds of the galaxy, less and less gas remains to compose the next generation of stars. Eventually the gas supply will run out, as it already has in nearly half the galaxies in the universe. The small fraction of stars with the highest mass collapse completely, never to be seen again. Some stars end their lives by blowing their guts across the galaxy in a supernova explosion. This returned gas can then be tapped for the next generation. But the majority of stars—the Sun included—ultimately exhaust the fuel at their cores, and after the bulbous giant phase, collapse to form a compact orb of matter that radiates its feeble leftover heat to the frigid universe.

The complete list of corpses may sound familiar: black holes, neutron stars (pulsars), white dwarfs, and even brown dwarfs are each a dead end on the evolutionary tree of stars. What they each have in common is an eternal lock on cosmic construction materials. In other words, if stars burn out and no new ones are formed to replace them, then the universe will eventually contain no living stars.

How about Earth? We rely on the Sun for a daily infusion of energy to sustain life. If the Sun and the energy from all other stars were cut off from us, then mechanical and chemical processes (life included) on and within Earth would "wind down." Eventually, the energy of all motion gets lost to friction and the system reaches a single uniform temperature. This would really be bad. The starless Earth will lie naked in the presence of the frozen background of the expanding universe. The temperature on Earth will drop the way a freshly baked pie cools on a windowsill. Yet Earth is not alone in this fate. Trillions of years into the future, when all stars are gone and every process in every nook and cranny of the expanding universe has wound down, all parts of the cosmos will cool to the same temperature as the ever-cooling background. At that time, space travel will no longer provide refuge. Even hell will have frozen over. We may then declare that the universe has died—not with a bang but with a whimper.

# GOD AND THE ASTRONOMERS

## A SEARCH FOR MEANING IN THE COSMOS

FOR NEARLY EVERY PUBLIC LECTURE THAT I GIVE on the universe, I try to reserve adequate time for questions at the end. The progression of subjects raised is predictable. First, the questions relate directly to the lecture. They next migrate to sexy astrophysical subjects such as black holes, quasars, and the big bang. If I have enough time at the end to answer an unlimited number of questions, the subject eventually reaches God. Typical questions asked of me include "Do scientists believe in God?" "Do you believe in God?" "Do your studies in astrophysics make you more or less religious?"

Publishers have come to learn that there is a lot of money in God, and the "greatest story ever told," especially when the author is a scientist and when the book title includes the juxtaposition of scientific and religious themes. Successful books include Robert Jastrow's *God and the Astronomers*, Leon M. Lederman's *The God Particle*, Frank J. Tipler's *The Physics of Immortality: Modern Cosmology, God, and the Resurrection of the Dead*, and Paul Davies's two works *God and the New Physics* and *The Mind of God: The Scientific Basis for a Rational World*. Each author is either an accomplished physicist or astronomer, and while the books are not strictly religious, they bring God into conversations about astrophysics. Even Stephen Jay Gould, a Darwinian pitbull and devout agnostic, has joined the title parade with his work *Rock of Ages: Science and Religion in the Fullness of Life*. The commercial success of these books indicates that there is a hungry audience that seeks answers that bridge the chasm between science and religion.

Journalists are not immune from this movement. When the structure within the cosmic microwave background radiation was discovered by the satellite known as the Cosmic Background Explorer, the principal investigator of the project tried to impress upon the media the significance of the result to modern cosmology. He simply said, "If you are religious, it's like seeing God." Not losing an opportunity to quote a scientist who invokes the name of God, the press swiftly misquoted the statement with banner headlines that blared, "Astronomers Discover God" and "Astronomers See the Face of God."

After the publication of *The Physics of Immortality*, which explored whether the laws of physics could allow you and your soul to exist long after you are gone from this world, Frank J. Tipler's book tour included many well-paid lectures to Protestant religious groups. This science-God movement has further blossomed in recent years with efforts made by Sir John Templeton, the wealthy founder of the Templeton investment fund, to find harmony and consilience between science and religion. Apart from sponsoring workshops and conferences on the subject, Templeton occasionally targets widely published religion-friendly scientists for an annual award whose cash value rivals that of the Nobel prize.

Let there be no doubt that as they are currently practiced, science and religion enjoy no common ground. As was thoroughly documented in the nineteenth-century tome *A History of the Warfare of Science with Theology in Christendom*, by the historian and onetime president of Cornell University Andrew D. White, history reveals a long and combative relationship between religion and science, depending on who was in control of society at the time. The claims of science rely on experimental verification, while the claims of religions rely on faith. These are irreconcilable approaches to knowing, which ensures an eternity of debate wherever and whenever the two camps meet. Just as in hostage negotiations, it's probably best to keep both sides talking to each other. But the schism did not come about for want of earlier attempts to bring the two sides together.

Great scientific minds, from Claudius Ptolemy of the second century to Isaac Newton of the seventeenth, invested their formidable intellects in attempts to deduce the nature of the universe from the statements and philosophies contained in religious writings. Indeed, by the time of his death, in 1727, Newton had penned more words about God and religion than about the laws of physics, all in a futile attempt to use biblical chronology to understand and predict events in the natural world. Had any of these efforts worked, science and religion today might be one and the same.

But they are not.

The argument is simple. I have yet to see a successful prediction about the physical world that was inferred extrapolated from the information content of any religious document. Indeed, I can make an even stronger statement. Whenever people have used religious documents to make accurate predictions about our base knowledge of the physical world they have been famously wrong. Note that a scientific prediction, which is a precise statement about the untested behavior of objects or phenomena in the natural world, should be logged *before* the event takes place. When your model predicts something only after it happened then you have instead made a "postdiction." Postdictions comprise the backbone of most creation myths and, of course, of the *Just So* stories of Rudyard Kipling, where explanations of everyday phenomena account for what is already known. In the business of science, however, a hundred postdictions are hardly worth a single successful prediction.

Topping the list of failed predictions are the perennial claims about when the world will end, none of which has yet proved true. But other claims and predictions have actually stalled or reversed the progress of science. We find a leading example in the trial of Galileo (which gets my vote for the trial of the millennium) where he showed the universe to be fundamentally different from the dominant views of the Catholic Church. In all fairness to the Inquisition, however, an Earth-centered universe made a lot of sense observationally. With a full complement of epicycles to explain the peculiar motions of the planets against the background stars, the time-honored, Earth-centered model had conflicted with no known observations. This remained true long after Copernicus introduced his Sun-centered model of the universe a century earlier.

The Earth-centric model was also aligned with the teachings of the Catholic Church and prevailing interpretations of the Bible, wherein Earth is unambiguously created before the Sun and the Moon as described in the first several verses of Genesis. If you were created first, then you must be in the center of all motion. Where else could you be? Furthermore, the Sun and the Moon themselves were also presumed to be smooth orbs. Why would a perfect, omniscient deity create anything else?

All this changed, of course, with the invention of the telescope and Galileo's observations of the heavens. The new optical device revealed aspects of the cosmos that strongly conflicted with people's conceptions of an Earth-centered, blemish-free, divine universe. The Moon's surface was bumpy and rocky. The Sun's surface had spots that moved across its surface; Jupiter had moons of its own that orbited Jupiter and not Earth; and Venus went through phases, just like the moon. For his radical discoveries, which shook the Christian world, Galileo's books were banned, and he was put on trial, found guilty of heresy, and sentenced to house arrest. This was benign punishment when one considers what happened to the monk Giordano Bruno. A few decades earlier, Bruno had been found guilty of heresy and burned at the stake for suggesting that Earth may not be the only place in the universe that harbors life.

I do not mean to imply that competent scientists, soundly conducting the scientific method, have not also been famously wrong. They have. Most scientific claims made on the frontier will ultimately be disproved, usually with the arrival of more or better data. But this scientific method, which allows for expeditions down intellectual dead ends, also promotes ideas, models, and predictive theories that can be spectacularly correct. No other enterprise in the history of human thought has been as successful at decoding the ways and means of the universe.

Scientists are occasionally accused by others of being closed-minded or stubborn. Often people make such accusations when they see scientists swiftly discount astrology, the paranormal, Sasquatch sightings, and other areas of human interest that routinely fail double-blind tests or that possess a dearth of reliable evidence. But this same level of skepticism also gets levied upon ordinary scientific claims in the professional research journals. The standards are the same. Look what happened when the Utah chemists B. Stanley Pons and Martin Fleischmann claimed in a press conference to create "cold" nuclear fusion on their laboratory table. Scientists acted swiftly and skeptically. Within days of the announcement it became clear that no one could replicate the cold fusion results that Pons and Fleischmann claimed for their experiment. Their work was summarily dismissed. Similar plot lines unfold almost daily (minus the press conferences) for nearly every new scientific claim.

With scientists exhibiting such strong levels of skepticism, some people may be surprised to learn we heap our largest rewards and praises upon colleagues who succeed in discovering flaws in accepted paradigms. These same rewards also go to those who create new ways to understand the universe. Nearly all famous scientists—pick your favorite one—have been so praised in their own lifetime. This path to success in one's professional career is antithetical to almost every other human establishment—especially to religion.

None of this is to say that the world does not contain religious scientists. In a survey of religious beliefs among math and science professionals,* 65 percent of the mathematicians (the highest rate) declared themselves to be religious, as did 22 percent of the physicists and astronomers (the lowest rate). The national average among all scientists was around 40 percent and has remained largely unchanged over the past century. For reference, 90 percent of the American public claims to be religious (among the highest in Western society), so either nonreligious people are drawn to science or studying science makes you less religious.

But what of those scientists who are religious? One thing is for sure: Successful researchers do not get their science from religious doctrines. But the methods of science have little or nothing to contribute to ethics, inspiration, morals, beauty, love, hate, or social mores. These are vital elements to civilized life, about which God in nearly every religion has much to say. For many scientists there is no conflict of interest.

When scientists do talk about God, they typically invoke him at the boundaries of knowledge where we are most humble and where our sense of wonder is greatest. Examples of this abound. During an era when planetary motions were on the frontier of natural philosophy, Ptolemy couldn't help feeling a religious sense of majesty when he penned,

---

*Edward J. Larson & Larry Wiham, *Nature* (April 3, 1997).

*When I trace at my pleasure the windings to and
fro of the heavenly bodies, I no longer touch the
earth with my feet. I stand in the presence of Zeus
himself and take my fill of ambrosia.*

Note that Ptolemy was not weepy about the fact that the element mercury is liquid at room temperature, or that a
dropped rock falls straight to the ground. While he could not
have fully understood these phenomena either, they were not
seen at the time to be on the frontiers of science and worthy
of a religious epithet.

In the thirteenth century, Alfonso the Wise (Alfonso X), the
King of Castile and León, who also happened to be an accomplished academician, was frustrated by the complexity of
Ptolemy's epicycles. Being less humble than Ptolemy, Alfonso
is credited with having mused, "Had I been around at the creation, I would have given some useful hints for the better or-
dering of the universe."

In his 1687 masterpiece, *The Mathematical Principles of
Natural Philosophy*, Isaac Newton lamented that his new equations of gravity, which describe the force of attraction between
pairs of objects, would not maintain a stable system of orbits
for multiple planets. Under this instability, planets would either
crash into the Sun or get ejected from the solar system alto-
gether. Worried about the long-term fate of Earth and other
planets, Newton invoked the hand of God as a restoring force
that would maintain a long-lived solar system. Over a century
later, the French mathematician and dynamicist Pierre-Simon
de Laplace invented perturbation theory for his five-volume
treatise *Celestial Mechanics* (1799–1825), which, as noted ear-

lier, extended the applicability of Newton's equations to complex systems of planets such as ours. Laplace showed that our solar system was indeed stable and did not require the hand of a deity after all. When queried by Napoléon Bonaparte on the absence of any reference to an "author of the universe" in his book, Laplace replied, "I have no need of that hypothesis."

And in full agreement with King Alfonso's frustrations with the universe, Albert Einstein noted in a letter to a colleague, "If God created the world, his primary worry was certainly not to make its understanding easy for us." When Einstein could not figure out how or why a deterministic universe would require the roulette formalisms of quantum mechanics, he grumbled, "It is hard to sneak a look at God's cards. But that he would choose to play dice with the world . . . is something that I cannot believe for a single moment." When an experimental result was shown to Einstein that would have disproved his new theory of gravity, Einstein commented, "The Lord is subtle, but malicious he is not." The Danish physicist Niels Bohr, a contemporary of Einstein's, heard one too many of Einstein's God remarks and declared that Einstein should stop telling God what to do!

Today, you hear the occasional astrophysicist (one in fifty or so) invoke God when asked where all our laws of physics came from, or what was around before the big bang. As we have come to anticipate, these questions comprise the modern frontier of cosmic discovery, and at the moment (like the above examples in their day), they transcend the answers our available data can supply. Some promising ideas already exist that address these questions, such as inflationary cosmology and string theory. They may ultimately provide the answers, pushing back the boundary of our awe of the cosmos.

My personal views are entirely pragmatic, and partly resonate with those of Galileo who, during his trial, is credited with saying, "The Bible tells you how to go to heaven, not how the heavens go." Galileo further noted, in a 1615 letter to Madame Christina of Lorraine, the Grand Duchess of Tuscany, "In my mind God wrote two books. The first book is the Bible, where humans can find the answers to their questions on values and morals. The second book of God is the book of nature, which allows humans to use observation and experiment to answer our own questions about the universe."

I simply go with what works. And what works is the healthy skepticism embodied in the scientific method. Believe me, if the Bible had ever been shown to be a rich source of scientific answers and enlightenment, we would be mining it daily for cosmic discovery. Yet my vocabulary of scientific inspiration strongly overlaps with that of religious enthusiasts. I, like Ptolemy, am humbled in the presence of our clockwork universe. When I am on the cosmic frontier, and I touch the laws of physics with my pen, or when I look upon the endless sky from an observatory on a mountaintop, I well up with an admiration for its splendor. But I do so knowing and accepting that if I propose a God beyond that horizon, one who graces the valley of our collective ignorance, then the day will come again when our sphere of knowledge has grown so large that I will have "no need of that hypothesis."

I will have no need because science has a "greatest story ever told" of its own, and the story gets greater by the day:

In the beginning, sometime between twelve and sixteen billion years ago, all the space and all the matter and all the energy of the known universe was contained in a volume smaller than the head of a pin. Conditions were so hot, the basic forces of nature that collectively describe the universe were unified. For reasons unknown, this pinhead cosmos began to expand. When at its dawn the universe was a piping-hot 1,000,000,000,000,000,000,000,000,000,000 degrees Celsius, and a mere 0.00000000000000000000000000000000000000001 seconds old—before which all of our theories of matter and space break down and have no meaning—black holes spontaneously formed, disappeared, and formed again out of the energy contained within the unified field.

Under these extreme conditions, in what is admittedly speculative physics, the structure of space and time became severely curved as it gurgled into a spongy, foamlike structure. During this epoch, phenomena described by Einstein's general theory of relativity (the modern theory of gravity) and quantum mechanics (the description of matter on its smallest scales) were indistinguishable. As the universe continued to expand and cool, gravity became the first to split from the other forces and attain a separate identity. Quickly thereafter, the strong nuclear force and the electroweak force split from each other, which was accompanied by an enormous release of stored energy that induced a rapid, thirty-power-of-ten increase in the size of the universe. The rapid expansion of the universe, known as the epoch of inflation, stretched and smoothed out the cosmic distribution of matter and energy so that any regional variation in density became less than one part in one hundred thousand—a ripple the height of one tenth of a millimeter in an Olympic-size swimming pool.

Continuing onward with what is now laboratory-confirmed physics, the universe was hot enough for photons of light to spontaneously convert their energy into matter-antimatter particle pairs, which immediately thereafter annihilated each other, returning their energy back to photons. For reasons unknown, this symmetry between matter and antimatter had been "broken" at the previous force splitting, which led to a slight excess of matter over antimatter. This asymmetry was small but crucial to the future evolution of the universe: For every billion antimatter particles, a billion +1 matter particles were born.

As the universe continued to cool, the electroweak force split into the electromagnetic force and the weak nuclear force, completing the four distinct and familiar forces of nature. While the energy of the photon bath continued to drop, pairs of matter-antimatter particles could no longer be created spontaneously from the available photons. All remaining pairs of matter-antimatter particles swiftly annihilated, leaving behind a universe with one particle of ordinary matter for every billion photons—and no antimatter. Had this matter-over-antimatter asymmetry not emerged, the expanding universe would forever be composed of light and nothing else, not even astrophysicists.

Over a roughly four-minute period, protons and neutrons assembled from the annihilations to become the simplest atomic nuclei. Meanwhile, free-roving electrons thoroughly scattered the photons to and fro, creating an opaque soup of matter and energy. When the universe cooled below a few thousand degrees Kelvin—about the temperature of fireplace embers—the loose electrons moved slowly enough to get snatched from the soup by the roving nuclei to make complete atoms of hydrogen, helium, and lithium, the three lightest elements.

The universe is now (for the first time) transparent to visible light, and these free-flying photons are visible today as the cosmic microwave background. Over the first billion years, the universe continued to expand and cool as matter gravitated into the massive concentrations we call galaxies. Between fifty and a hundred billion of them formed, each containing hundreds of billions of stars that undergo thermonuclear fusion in their cores. Those stars with more than about ten times the mass of the Sun achieve sufficient pressure and temperature in their cores to manufacture dozens of elements heavier than hydrogen, including the elements that compose planets and the life upon them. These elements would be embarrassingly useless were they to remain locked inside the star. But high-mass stars fortuitously explode, scattering their chemically enriched guts throughout the galaxy.

After seven or eight billion years of such enrichment, an undistinguished star (the Sun) was born in an undistinguished region (the Orion Arm) of an undistinguished galaxy (the Milky Way) in an undistinguished part of the universe (the outskirts of the Virgo supercluster). The gas cloud from which the Sun formed contained a sufficient supply of heavy elements to spawn a system of nine planets, thousands of asteroids, and billion of comets. During the formation of this star system, matter condensed and accreted out of the parent cloud of gas while circling the Sun.

For several hundred million years, the persistent impact of high-velocity comets and other leftover debris rendered the surfaces of the rocky planets molten and sterile, preventing the formation of complex molecules. As less and less accretable matter remained in the solar system, the planet surfaces began to cool. The one we call Earth formed in a zone around the Sun where oceans remain largely in liquid form. Had Earth been much closer to the Sun, the oceans would have vaporized. Had Earth been much farther, the oceans would have frozen over. In either case, life as we know it would not have emerged.

Within the chemically rich liquid oceans, by a mechanism unknown, there emerged simple anaerobic bacteria that unwittingly transformed Earth's carbon dioxide–rich atmosphere into one with sufficient oxygen to allow aerobic organisms to evolve and dominate the oceans and land. These same oxygen atoms, normally found in pairs ($O_2$) also combined in threes to form ozone ($O_3$) in the upper atmosphere, which served (and continues to serve) as a shield that protects Earth's surface from most of the Sun's molecule-hostile ultraviolet photons. The remarkable diversity of life on Earth, and we presume elsewhere in the universe, is owed to the cosmic abundance of carbon and the countless number of molecules (simple and complex) made from it. How can you argue when there are more varieties of carbon-based molecules than all other molecules combined. But life is fragile.

Earth's encounters with large, leftover meteors, a formerly common event, wreak intermittent havoc upon the ecosystem. A mere sixty-five million years ago (less than 2 percent of Earth's past), a ten-trillion-ton asteroid hit what is now the Yucatán Peninsula and obliterated over 70 percent of Earth's flora and fauna—including dinosaurs, the dominant land animals. This ecological tragedy pried open an opportunity for small surviving mammals to fill freshly vacant niches. One big-brained branch of these mammals, the one we call primates, evolved a genus and species (*Homo sapiens*) to a level of intelligence that enabled them to invent the methods and tools of science. They then invented astrophysics and went on to deduce the origin and evolution of the universe.

Yes, the universe had a beginning. Yes, the universe continues to evolve. And yes, each of our body's atoms can be traced to the big bang and to the thermonuclear furnace within high-mass stars. We are not simply in the universe, we are part of it. We are born from it. One might even say life has been empowered by the universe to figure itself out.

In the cycle of life, the total of all matter and energy remains unchanged—a fundamental feature of physical laws that falls closest to my heart. I have even taken the concept to a level of which the New Age movement would be proud. When I die, I want to be buried, not cremated. Whenever you burn organic matter, including human corpses, the chemical energy content of the body's quadrillion cells converts entirely into heat energy, which raises the atmospheric temperature near the crematorium, and eventually radiates back into space. When deposited into the universe, this low energy thermal radiation increases cosmic entropy and is largely unrecoverable to perform any further work.

I owe Earth (and the universe) much more than this. For my entire omnivorous life I have eaten of its flora and feasted on its fauna. Countless plants and animals have sacrificed their lives and unwillingly donated their energy content to my sustenance. The least I can do is donate my body back to this third rock from the Sun. I want to be buried, just like in the old days, where I decompose by the action of microorganisms, and I am dined upon by any form of creeping animal, or root system that sees fit to do so. I would become their food, just as they had been food for me. I will have recycled back to the universe at least some of the energy that I have taken from it. And in so doing, at the conclusion of my scientific adventures, I will have come closer to the heavens than to Earth.

# APPENDIX

SPACE-TIME CONTINUUM

## A CHRONICLE OF LIFE'S MINUTIAE

BORN NEIL DE GRASSE TYSON, Sunday, 5 October 1958, Mount Sinai Hospital, Manhattan, a year and a day after the Soviet Union successfully launched *Sputnik*. Others born in 1958 include the pop singer–performers Madonna, The Artist Formerly Known as Prince, and Michael Jackson. Other notable 1958ers include Caroline Kennedy, the International Geophysical Year, the Barbie Doll, and NASA.

Lived from age 0 to age 17 as a resident of the Bronx, New York City.

**1963/64:** Attended Public School 36 (PS-36) in the Castle Hill section of the East Bronx for kindergarten.

**1964:** Moved to Riverdale (northwest Bronx) and attended PS-81 from 1st through 6th grade.

**1966 (Fall):** First visit to the Hayden Planetarium.

**1968:** While away at summer camp, I was voted the camp Olympian for exceptional athletic performance during the end-of-year athletic festivities.

**1968/69:** Elected class president (5th grade).

**1968/69:** Am thrilled by brainteaser books.

**1969:** While away at summer camp, for a second year in a row I was voted camp Olympian.

**1969:** Looked through binoculars at the sky for the first time.

**1969:** My 6th-grade science teacher recommended that I take astronomy courses at the Hayden Planetarium.

**1969/70:** Elected class president (6th grade).

**1969:** Joined the neighborhood Little League baseball team. I was a catcher, and batted cleanup.

**1970:** Playing for the same Little League team the following year, I led the league in stolen bases and slugging percentage. My team won the division. I played on the all-star team.

**1970:** Won gold swimming medals at the annual swimming meet at the neighborhood pool.

**1970:** Won track medals in the sprint races at the annual Public School Athletic League (PSAL) district track meet.

**1970/71:** Moved to Lexington, Massachusetts, for one year. Lived in a suburban home for the first time.

One of three Black children in the school (student body approx. 600).

**1971:** Returned to the Bronx. Attended Junior High School 141 for grades 8 and 9.

**1971/72:** Walked dogs for extra money.

**1972:** Constructed from scratch a prism spectroscope for the school science fair.

**1972 (Fall):** During an advanced astronomy course at the Hayden Planetarium, met the Education Director of the New York Explorers Club.

**1973 (April):** Slam-dunked a basketball for the first time. 9th Grade, my height: 5′ 9″.

**1973 (June):** Graduation night Junior High School graduating class took the Circle Line boat ride around Manhattan. Simultaneously, I boarded the *S.S. Canberra* in the adjacent pier, to begin a trip to the northwest coast of Africa to view and photograph a total solar eclipse.

**1973 (August):** Attended Camp Uraniborg, a summer astronomy camp in the Mojave Desert.

**1973 (September):** Admitted to the Bronx High School of Science for grades 10, 11, and 12.

**1973 (October):** Gave the first formal lecture of my life (age 15).

**1974 (Spring):** Designated "Gifted and Talented" by the U.S. Department of Education Office of the Gifted and Talented.

**1974 (Summer):** Traveled to Scotland on expedition with a team of scientists and students.

**1975 (June):** Got the highest score in the school for the statewide Mathematics Regents Exam.

**1975 (Summer):** Became a lifeguard and worked at Westchester's Dunwoodie Day Camp for inner-city children. I also worked at a neighborhood pool.

**1975/76:** Editor in chief of the *Physical Science Journal* of the Bronx High School of Science.

**1975/76:** Captain of the wrestling team. Undefeated (10–0). All but one victory ended in a pin.

**1976 (June):** Graduated from the Bronx High School of Science.

**1976 (September):** Left NYC to attend Harvard University. I unknowingly and swiftly lost my New York City accent.

**1976 (Fall):** Rowed freshman crew. Achieved the highest rowing-machine score among five years of freshman rowers.

**1977 (Spring):** Disillusioned with the rowing culture, I return to wrestling. Had a losing record until my senior year.

**1977/78:** I tutored convicted felons in mathematics at Walpole State Penitentiary, New England's maximum security prison.

**1978/79:** Danced with Expressions Dance Company. Style: jazz, ballet, Afro-Caribbean.

**1980:** Earned varsity letter in wrestling. Elected to the Harvard Varsity Club.

**1980 (June):** Graduated from Harvard with a B.A. in physics.

**1980 (August):** Left Harvard to attend graduate school at the University of Texas.

**1982:** Began to write for the popular-level astronomy magazine *Stardate*. My Q&A column ultimately becomes the basis for two books. My essays for *Stardate* will also form the basis for a book.

**1983:** Danced with Inner Visions Dance Company. Style: jazz, Afro-Caribbean.

**1983 (May):** Earned the M.A. in astronomy from the University of Texas with a 130-page thesis.

**1984:** Published my first (coauthored) research paper in a refereed journal.

**1984/85:** Danced with the University of Texas Dance Team. Styles: Latin ballroom, ballet, jazz.

**1985:** Won a gold medal with the U.T. Dance Team in team competition at a national tournament in Glendale, California. Style: International Latin ballroom.

**1986:** Averaged $6,000 per year for the previous four years in revenue from speaking fees and popular-level writing. Built a collection of fine wines with the monies.

**1987:** Left Texas to teach for one year at the University of Maryland's Department of Astronomy.

**1988:** Published my first solo-authored research paper in the *Astrophysical Journal*.

**1988:** Left Maryland to continue graduate school at Columbia University.

**1988 (September):** Married Alice of Fairbanks, Alaska—a Ph.D. mathematical physicist whom I met in 1980 in Austin at the University of Texas. We married at a church in Harlem, with a reception at the New York Botanical Gardens in the Bronx.

**1989 (October):** Published *Merlin's Tour of the Universe* with Columbia Press. Very likely the first book on the universe by a Black author since Benjamin Banneker published his annual *Almanac*, begun in 1792.

**1990/91:** *Merlin's Tour of the Universe* was translated into Japanese (Tokyo) and Spanish (Mexico City).

**1991 (May):** Earned the M.Phil. and Ph.D. in astrophysics. Thesis is 285 pages. Selected by the dean to deliver the Ph.D. convocation address at graduation.

**1991:** Left Columbia to become a postdoctoral research associate at Princeton University's Department of Astrophysics.

**1992 (February):** Invited (all expenses paid) to present a research paper at an astrophysics conference in Capetown, South Africa—two months before the election that formally abolished apartheid.

**1993:** Elected to the Board of Directors of the Astronauts Memorial Foundation (AMF), Cape Canaveral, Florida. I am the youngest member of the board by ten years.

**1994 (May):** Published *Universe Down to Earth* with Columbia Press.

**1994 (July):** Promoted to member of the research staff at Princeton simultaneously with obtaining a joint appointment with the Hayden Planetarium of the American Museum of Natural History. We begin planning a complete reconstruction of the Hayden Planetarium—a plan that would ultimately cost over $200 million and reclaim Hayden's preeminence as the leading planetarium in the world.

**1994 (July):** Delivered the keynote luncheon address at the dedication of the AMF Center for Space Education at the Kennedy Space Center.

**1995 (June):** Promoted to acting director of the Hayden Planetarium.

**1996 (May):** Promoted to the Frederick P. Rose Director of the Hayden Planetarium.

**1996:** Contracted with Doubleday to produce three books: (1) Reprint of *Merlin's Tour of the Universe*, (2) sequel to Merlin: *Just Visiting This Planet*, and, of course, (3) *The Sky Is Not the Limit*.

**1997 (January):** Hayden Planetarium closes for demolition and construction.

**2000 (Spring):** The most ambitious facility for astronomy education ever conceived, The Rose Center for Earth and Space, containing the rebuilt Hayden Planetarium, opens to the public.

# ACKNOWLEDGMENTS

OF THE HUNDREDS OF PEOPLE WHO have been there for me over the years, I single out my wife, Alice, my father, Cyril, my mother, Sunchita, my brother, Stephen Sr., and my sister, Lynn. Through their continual love and support, they have collectively supplied an emotional and intellectual buoyancy to my life's journeys. By way of their advice, wisdom, and guidance I have cleared life's hurdles and survived life's challenges. For this, I owe them more than I have the capacity to express.

Betsy Lerner, my editor, has supported my writings and has observed my career since my later years in graduate school. She alone encouraged me to write this memoir and I am thankful for her persistence, in spite of my stubborn apprehensions about undertaking such a project.

Portions of chapters 4 and 6 are adapted from essays that touched upon my life and appeared in *Natural History* magazine under my column "Universe."